THE HUMAN
CONNECTION

THE HUMAN CONNECTION

Ashley Montagu and
Floyd Matson

McGRAW-HILL BOOK COMPANY
New York St. Louis San Francisco Bogotá Guatemala
Hamburg Lisbon Madrid Mexico Montreal Panama
Paris San Juan São Paulo Tokyo Toronto

To the memory of Howard Gossage

1 2 3 4 5 6 7 8 9 FG FG 8 7 6 5 4 3 2 1 0

LIBRARY OF CONGRESS CATALOGING IN PUBLICATION DATA
Montagu, Ashley, date
  The human connection.
  Includes index.
  1. Communication.   I. Matson, Floyd W., joint
author.   II. Title.
P90.M545   301.2'1   79-1411
ISBN 0-07-042840-9
0-07-042842-5 (paperback)
Book design by Lynn Braswell

CONTENTS

| INTRODUCTION

There is more than a verbal tie between the words common, community, and communication. Men live in a community by virtue of the things which they have in common; and communication is the way in which they come to possess things in common. . . . Consensus demands communication.

—John Dewey

Communication is the name we give to the countless ways that humans have of keeping in touch—not just to words and music, pictures and print, but also to cries and whispers, nods and becks, postures and plumages: to every move that catches someone's eye and every sound that resonates upon another ear. Human communication, as the saying goes, is a clash of symbols; and it covers a multitude of signs. But it is more than media and messages, information and persuasion; it also meets a deeper need and serves a higher purpose. Whether clear or garbled, tumultuous or silent, deliberate or fatally inadvertent, communication is the ground of meeting and the foundation of community. It is, in short, the essential human connection.

All too often, of course, that connection is broken—as much from ignorance as from malice, through gestures of indifference as well as acts of sabotage. Between persons or between cultures, it is always difficult to make contact without colliding. In our technotronic age, as distances dissolve and spaces shrink around us, there is no lack of contact and "confrontation" (the harmless word has become a synonym for standoff), but there is a pervasively felt absence of genuine communication—of getting through and coming across, of being heard or gaining a response, of achieving friendship or experiencing love. As David Riesman observed a generation ago, it is lonely in the crowd. We keep calling, but the line is busy. We advance, but we are not recognized. And so we retreat, more and more, into the fantasy of companionship and conviviality—the facsimile of communion—provided for us by the Magic Theater of electric enlightenment. Surrounded by the massed media, thoroughly penetrated by their cosmetic rays, saturated with information and entirely persuaded, still we feel ourselves unaddressed and unknown. Our identity seems reduced to that of occupant.

In the face-to-face contacts of everyday life, much as in our faceless encounters with the media, there is a scarcity of mutual recognition and genuine dialogue. The two realms of communication are alike in that; but there is a crucial difference between them. For in the drama of everyday life, unlike that of the Magic Theater, it is we who are the actors—in the double sense both of performing roles and of carrying out actions. Here we write the script and improvise the moves; and because it is a social world through which we move, every action has the character of a transaction and every private expression conveys a public impression. In the service of our ongoing career through the world of others, we call upon an elaborate repertoire of communicative resources, with a display of ingenuity and versatility rivaling that of the most proficient artists and craftsmen. We alternate "channels" and mix sensory effects like expert technicians; we execute delicate bodily maneuvers and choreograph our gestures with the rhythmic grace of dancers; we change roles, put on and take off masks, and stage our continuous performances like the most gifted of actors. And we are masters of sign language, possessing a kinesic vocabulary of extraordinary depth and range. Some part of our dexterity in communication is inborn, the product of evolutionary adaptation; by far the greater part is learned, the product of cultural transmission—though the learning is informal and the performance largely unconscious.

This portrayal of the artful and sensuous enterprise of human communication is not, to be sure, the traditional view of the subject. Until very recently the systematic study of communication was heavily dominated by the verbal and logical bias of Western culture—that "Gutenberg Galaxy" delineated by Marshall McLuhan which took its cue from the linear pattern of words in print and elaborated a no-nonsense theory of communication as the simple transmission of information from A to B. If B got the message, that was "good communication"; anything else that might transpire between the two human points, such as the twitching of bodies or the emission of sighs, was regarded as interference or "noise"—that is, "bad communication." In effect there was only one sensory channel (the audio-acoustic) and only one medium (speech) through which human beings could make any meaningful contact with one another.

That is no longer the case in the study of communication. By virtue of a remarkable series of discoveries and departures in the social sciences—substantial enough to be heralded as a "new look" and "new wave"—our understanding of the process of communication has been not only expanded but virtually transformed. Contributions to the new look have come from such different fields as sociology, anthropology, psychology, biology, and philosophy—which together have spun off a host of lively specialties devoted to the subject of social interaction. Among them are kinesics—the study of body motion, also called body language; proxemics—the study of the communicative aspects of the cultural patterning of space between people; ethnomethodology; phenomenology; human ecology; and humanistic psychology. In each case the direction of interest is conspicuously away from traditional preoccupations. Where once the study of social behavior was typically formalistic, abstract, and statistical, today it is increasingly informal, naturalistic, and common-sensical. And where, in the study of communication, the emphasis was predominantly on the spoken or written word (under such rubrics as linguistics, semantics, rhetoric, and logic), it is now significantly nonverbal. For example, linguistics has been modified by paralinguistics, which is the study of such human communicative sounds as tone of voice, hesitations, snickers, groans, sighs, belches, drawling, and clipped speech—sounds that convey the speaker's emotional or subjective stance or a culturally defined message, as does clearing the throat. In like fashion, semantics has been modified by kinesics and proxemics, and logic and rhetoric by phenomenology and the psychology of persuasion.

It is not merely a hidden dimension or a silent language that has been uncovered by the new wave of scientific explorers; it is more like a neglected universe of discourse and intercourse. We are becoming aware that the verbal domain is only the tip of the iceberg of communicative experience—that there is more, much more, to the human dialogue than meets the ear. While speech and language have not diminished in importance, they have been newly situated on a broader and richer canvas, enlivened by colors and textures never noticed before. The process of communication has acquired not only depth but dignity. No longer does it resemble a transmission belt mechanically conveying bits of information between detached entities inhabiting black boxes; rather it comes to be seen (within the framework of a shared culture) as a participative relationship, a joint endeavor involving give as well as take, geared to common understandings and synchronized by communal rhythms. The underlying conception, to be sure, is far from novel; it embodies what James Carey has called the "ritual" view of communication as opposed to the "transmission" view, and it has deep roots in both philosophy and religion. But it is new to the mainstream of social science and to the major tributaries of social thought.

The wider field of social interaction—the matrix of all communication—has also been rediscovered and reappraised following an extended period of neglect. This is not the place for an account of the strange disappearance of ordinary people and everyday life from the annals of social science; suffice it to say that for several academic generations the dominant schools of social thought distinctly preferred the orderly to the ordinary and thoroughly subordinated interactions to institutions. To put it more directly, the prevailing view has—until only yesterday—been plainly skeptical toward common sense, indifferent to common experience, and at least a little suspicious of common men and women. And it is here that the new look in social science is most evidently in opposition; for its fundamental commitment is to the reasonableness of common sense and the trustworthiness of common experience. More specifically, it takes the everyday world to be the real world, and it goes so far as to choose the ordinary language as its own language. As Jack Douglas observes, "All of sociology necessarily begins with the understanding of everyday life. . . . Yet, until quite recently, few sociologists realized that the understanding of everyday life must be the foundation of all sociological research and theory; and fewer still acted in accord with this crucial fact."

Nor is this awareness limited to sociologists; a similar trend of thought has lately become manifest in such different fields as history and psychology. As historian Thomas R. Frazier has put it:

Most studies of history concentrate on public figures and public affairs, the events and people that most historians consider important or influential. What is left out in these traditional presentations is the ordinary, day-to-day life of most of the members of the given society—that is, the "private side" of history.

What is missing in the traditional study of history, moreover, is not just a lowly dimension of human existence; more important is the absence of any recognition that there were people out there, in whatever period, who were not simply enduring but acting on the world: making choices, forging careers, facing crises, managing grief, and consciously living their lives. The editors of another history reader, Burner, Marcus, and Tilson, note the impression given by American history textbooks with their standard accent on institutions: "Students come away with a shadowy vision of the people of the past 'responding' to the frontier, to industrialism, to the rise of a welfare state, and to the country's role in world politics. *The past becomes what happened to people, not what people did or who they were.*"

This rediscovery by historians of the forgotten private side or "underside" of history—what one scholar has called "the history of the inarticulate"—closely parallels a radical shift of priorities within psychology, commonly associated with humanistic and existential theorists, which has affirmed the value of conscious experience against the strictures of both behaviorism and Freudianism, and in so doing has upheld what might be termed the *normal* and *sociable* dimensions of ordinary human conduct.

The appreciation of the "normal" in particular distinguishes humanistic psychology from the classic tradition of psychoanalytic thought with its heavy stress on the "abnormal"; whereas for Freud the phenomena of everyday life fell within the category of psychopathology, for humanists such as Abraham Maslow these events are valued in themselves as expressions of personal experience in all its complexity and diversity—its peaks and valleys, ordinary pleasures and extraordinary yearnings, periods of constraint and moments of freedom.

This simultaneous recognition of the obvious, and collective rediscovery of the familiar, gives promise of bringing about something more than a passing flutter of intellectual fashion—more even than a corrective adjustment of scientific focus (from the abstract to the concrete). It presages nothing less than a transformation in the *image of man*—the implicit definition of human nature—which has held firm in the sciences of human behavior since their beginnings in the last century. That is the image which has relentlessly confined all of humankind within the determinate order of natural (and neutral) objects as described by the physical sciences. So long as the sciences of man have remained wedded to this derivative model, no other image could be conceived or nurtured in their laboratories than that of an inert and passive reactor, the "victim-spectator of forces working through him," in Gordon Allport's phrase—a creature devoid of reason or responsibility, beneath freedom and dignity, innately aggressive and insensibly driven, untouched and untouchable, unloving and unloved.

That may be the truth about us, after all. And in some ways, paradoxically, that monstrous image is easy to accept. It corresponds to the headlines; it reflects the situation tragedies playing daily on the tube; it defines the dark at the top of the stairs; it echoes our primal scream; and, in an odd but unmistakable way, it assuages our guilt. "For if we are all guilty," as the psychiatrist Frederic Wertham has said, "then none of us is guilty."

But that Hobbesian version of our natural state has nothing to say of other things we know about ourselves, have known in others, and dream impossibly to find again. What if it is not the true picture at all, but only the negative? It probes the winter of our discontent but misses the smiles of a summer's night; it seizes on the little murders and casual cruelties of our daily round but neglects our continuous small rescues. It knows nothing of friendship, for example, or of pleasant conversation; of dancing; or of a shared secret. And it denies love: that is its fatal unreality.

Some of these other things are in this book, which is concerned with the ordinary occurrences of everyday life; many of them are not here, because they do not bear observation well, being shy and private matters. But they are there nevertheless, behind the curtains, part of our lives and ourselves. Perhaps we may be permitted to glimpse them now and then, in these pages, and to acknowledge their presence.

1 | APPROACHING: Prologues, Proxemics, and Protocols

. . . She sat facing me with an older woman and a younger
And a little boy aged about five;
I could see that she was his mother,
Also she wore a wedding-ring and one set with diamonds.

She was about twenty-five years old,
Slim, graceful, disciplined;
She had none of the mannerisms of the suburbs,
No affectations, a low clear speech, good manners,
Hair thick and undyed.
She knew that she was beautiful and exceedingly attractive,
Every line of her dress showed it;
She was cool and determined and laughed heartily,
A wide mouth with magnificent teeth. . . .

She never showed a sign that she saw me
But I knew and she knew that I knew—
Our eyes fleeting past, never meeting directly
Like that vernal twinkling of butterflies
To which Coleridge compared Shakespeare's Venus and
Adonis.

—W. J. Turner, "Hymn to Her Unknown"

Face-to-face communication normally begins at extended visual distance, during the stage of *approach*—the prologue to meeting—when the participants come into mutual view and the internal mechanisms of person-perception, "checking up," and self-presentation are set in motion. Of course, it can be fully understood only in the context of the broader stream of events in which it takes place, but we can say nevertheless that approach may well be the most important, even crucial, phase of an encounter, from those transient episodes of casual mingling and bypassing where nothing more occurs, to the critical scenes of social life when "first impressions" matter most and when the act of approaching is elevated into "making an entrance." Everyday life no less than the theater has its entrances and exits, its approaches and withdrawals; and in the "drama of social reality" these framing moments are often essential to the play. The anxious ritual of approach rehearsed by T. S. Eliot's J. Alfred Prufrock reflects an apprehension familiar to many:

There will be time, there will be time
To prepare a face to meet the faces that you meet; . . .
And indeed there will be time
To wonder, "Do I dare?" and "Do I dare?"
Time to turn back and descend the stair,
With a bald spot in the middle of my hair—
(They will say: "How his hair is growing thin!")
My morning coat, my collar mounting firmly to the chin,
My necktie rich and modest, but asserted by a simple
pin—
(They will say: "But how his arms and legs are thin!")

It is ironic that this aspect of social behavior has been taken very seriously by nonacademic arbiters and counselors in the sociable arts, such as commercial advertisers and grooming stylists, while it has been traditionally ignored by the social sciences. The recent discovery by a new wave of social scientists of the everyday activity of self-presentation and "impression management" represents a belated recognition of a subject matter long familiar to dispensers and clients in the trades of fashion, cosmetics, and etiquette—all those for whom appearance is the true reality and "correct appearance" is the ultimate achievement. Advertisements for numerous products ranging from cars to underwear provide a continuous course of informal instruction in the delicate diplomacies of managing impressions and manipulating identities. Moreover, the most common scenarios enacted in these commercial mini-dramas ("I dreamed I was in Westminster Abbey in my Maiden-form Bra") center on strategies of approach, display, and self-advertisement. The apparent effectiveness of these ads suggests the widespread relevance and significance of their underlying themes.

THE EXPLORATION OF SPACE

Possibly the most important contribution to the understanding of human communication during the past two decades has been the virtually simultaneous recognition, within a wide range of disciplines, of the *uses of space*—by animals, by cultures, and by persons. Building on the earlier work of ethologists (such as H. E. Howard, Konrad Lorenz, and H. Hediger) with animals in their natural habitats, cultural anthropologists led by Edward T. Hall have adopted the label *proxemics* to cover "the interrelated observations and theories of man's use of space as a specialized elaboration of culture." Psychologists attuned to the influence of environment have introduced the subfield of ecological psychology, encompassing both the environmental conditions and social consequences of behavioral actions. "For example," as Roger Barker explains in *Ecological Psychology*, "ecological psychology deals not only with events involved in a player's catching a ball in a ball game, but also with the playing field [its size and shape], the other players [their number and skill], the rules of the game, and other ecological phenomena that affect the consequences for subsequent behavior of catching or not catching the ball."

Other social psychologists, such as Michael Argyle, have explored the personal and social uses of space as part of a wider interest in the nonverbal dimensions of social interaction. Microsociologists, following the lead of Erving Goffman, have identified spatial manipulation as a crucial factor in the negotiation of everyday encounters and relations in public space. Geographers, in the course of expanding (some would say "humanizing") their discipline to embrace both man-environment systems and "the spatial structure of human behavior," have thrown new light from their own standpoint on the cultural and personal ordering of space. Still another source of innovative thinking has come from the architectural and design professions, where researchers fol-

lowing Robert Sommer have emphasized the importance of spatial needs and manipulations as "the
behavioral basis of design."

It was Hall who originally addressed the questions
"How many distances do human beings have and
how do we distinguish them? What is it that differ-
entiates one distance from the other?" Beginning
with shifts in vocal volume (whispering at close distances, shouting at great distances), Hall detected a
series of eight distinct ranges of distance from "very
close" (participants three to six inches apart) all the
way to "stretching the limits of distance" (20 to 24
feet indoors, up to 100 feet outdoors). Later these
eight distances were reduced to four, which he
termed *intimate*, *personal*, *social*, and *public* (with each
having a close and far phase). The original observations and generalizations concerning the occupation
of these zones were made with middle-class white
Americans; but Hall's own extensive field work
abroad made him aware of the significant variations
between cultures, as well as of individual differences
within cultures. In *The Hidden Dimension* Hall hit on
the idea of a "situational personality" governing an
individual's style of performance in the transactions
associated with each of the four zones of distance.
"Some individuals never develop the public phase of
their personalities and, therefore, cannot fill public
spaces; they make very poor speakers or moderators.
As many psychiatrists know, other people have
trouble with the intimate and personal zones and
cannot endure closeness with others."

The key zone of interaction, for Hall and others
who have tracked the terrain, is that which charac-

terizes the normal spacing of members of the same species. Following the terminology of Hediger in his work with animals, Hall refers to this zone as personal distance (1½ to 4 feet apart) and distinguishes it on the one hand from intimate distance (0 to 18 inches)—"the distance of love-making and wrestling, comforting and protecting"—and on the other hand from the extended zones of social distance (4 to 12 feet) and public distance (12 to 25 feet or more), the margins of separation appropriate to business relations and public ceremonies respectively. Other students of spatial relations have rezoned the interpersonal landscape somewhat differently, or at least have changed the labels. Sommer, for example, uses "individual distance" in place of Hall's "personal distance" in order to distinguish that societywide zoning from the concept of "personal space," defined as a kind of psychic moat or protective bubble which each person carries with him as his own "portable territory . . . an area with invisible boundaries surrounding a person's body into which intruders may not come." In Sommer's view there are actually two defensive perimeters surrounding each of us: "The violation of individual distance is the violation of society's expectations; the invasion of personal space is an intrusion into a person's self-boundaries." A commonplace example of the latter is cited by Sommer in *Personal Space: The Behavioral Basis of Design:*

Dear Abby: I have a pet peeve that sounds so petty and stupid that I'm almost ashamed to mention it. It is people who come and sit down beside me on the piano bench while I'm playing. I don't know why this bothers me so much, but it does. Now you know, Abby, you can't tell someone to get up and go sit somewhere else without hurting their feelings. But it would be a big relief to me if I could get them to move in a nice inoffensive way. . . .

Lost Chord

Sommer's emphasis on the uniquely personal, private, and idiosyncratic uses of space has been questioned by other social scientists who point out that the setting of boundaries can be a flexible matter of negotiation between persons, varying according to the situation. Individuals who, for example, dislike sitting or standing very close to someone else when conversing may ride a jammed subway car or attend a crowded baseball game without a qualm.

Whether the critical factor governing the uses of space is personal, situational, cultural, biological, or a combination of all, there is no dispute among scientists that these manipulations are largely unconscious and of great significance both in interpreting social behavior and in the effort to improve communication, particularly between members of different cultures or ethnic groups. The anthropological investigations of Hall—as detailed in *The Silent Language* (1959), *The Hidden Dimension* (1966), and *Beyond Culture* (1976)—have especially called attention to the frustrations and confusions produced in cross-cultural encounters by these "out-of-awareness patterns" of spatial behavior. "As one travels abroad and examines the ways in which space is handled, startling variations are discovered—differences we react to vigorously. Since none of us is taught to look at space as isolated from other associations, feelings cued by the handling of space are often attributed to something else."

Ethologists have, for example, drawn a distinction between "contact" and "non-contact" species. Members of a "contact" culture or subculture generally touch one another more, face one another more directly, look one another in the eye more often, interact more closely, and speak more loudly than is characteristic of the members of a non-contact group. In the contact category are placed (among others) Latin Americans, Arabs, and southern Europeans; the non-contact group includes Asians, Indians and Pakistanis, northern Europeans, and Americans. According to Hall, "The 'non-contact' group perceives the contact group as overly familiar and sometimes 'pushy,' while the contact group refers to the non-contact as 'standoffish,' 'high-hat,' 'cold' or 'aloof.'" Comparing the behavior of Americans and Arabs in public places, for example, Hall observes that most Americans follow a tacit rule to the effect that "as soon as a person stops or is seated in a public place, there balloons around him a small sphere of privacy which is considered inviolate." On the other hand, "For the Arab, there is no such thing as an intrusion in public. Public means public." Therefore, an Arab may not only stand uncomfortably close to an American stranger but is likely to make every effort to maneuver and even push the other out of his place.

THE CULTURE OF PRIVACY

Clearly the meaning of personal privacy, as well as the valuation placed on it, varies widely from group to group. Even among the so-called non-contact peoples, such as those of northern Europe, variations in approaching and distancing are substantial and not always subtle. According to Hall, Germans are acutely sensitive to intrusions on the private sphere, both in architectural (fixed-feature) spaces such as offices and sitting rooms and in informal spaces such as conversational units. To an American, such overtures as standing on a threshold, talking through an open door, or poking one's head into another's room do not constitute intrusions or trespasses; but to a German they are likely to appear outrageous. "In every instance," says Hall, "where the American would consider himself *outside* he has already entered the German's territory and by definition would become involved with him." The German sensitivity to private space is said to be reflected in an insistence on individual rooms or cubicles, closed doors, and the maintenance of relatively rigid interpersonal distances in conversations and other transactions.

In contrast the Englishman of the middle or upper class, although his home is notoriously his castle, is less inclined to demand or expect a niche of his own and is accustomed to sharing space with others, largely as a result (according to Hall) of having been brought up in a nursery shared with brothers and sisters:

The difference between a room of one's own and early conditioning to shared space, while seeming inconsequential, has an important effect on the Englishman's attitude toward his own space. He may never have a permanent "room of his own" and seldom expects one or feels he is entitled to one. Even Members of Parliament have no offices and often conduct their business on the

terrace overlooking the Thames. . . . Americans working in England may become annoyed if they are not provided with what they consider appropriate enclosed work
space. In regard to the need for walls as a screen for the
ego, this places the Americans somewhere between the
Germans and the English.[1]

The recognition of spatial spheres of privacy, of
"personal bubbles" and individual preserves, has
been encouraged if not much enlightened by the cur-
rency given to the concept of "territoriality" by various students of animal behavior—notably the popular science writer Robert Ardrey. Although a few
social scientists have contended for a "zoological
perspective" involving a straightforward extrapolation of the presumed territorial instinct from animals
to men, most of those who employ the term regard it
simply as a useful metaphor to describe patterns of
behavior established not by instinct or imprinting
but by culture and learning.

In an important paper that first called attention to
the concept of territoriality as "a neglected sociological dimension," Stanford M. Lyman and Marvin B.
Scott distinguished four different kinds of territory
operative in human societies: "namely, *public territories, home territories, interactional territories* and *body
territories.*" Each of these demarcates a zone of encounter and communication, ranging downward
from the spacious to the intimate, in which unwritten rules of access and trespass, as well as formal
laws, function to impose boundaries that are commonly recognized by members of the culture. Thus
public territories are areas such as public parks and

beaches "where the individual has freedom of access, but not necessarily of action, by virtue of his claim to citizenship." Access itself may be curtailed where a public territory, such as a street corner or playground sector, has been defined by some as a home territory—a place "where the regular participants have a relative freedom of behavior and a sense of intimacy and control over the area." Examples cited by Lyman and Scott include children's clubhouses, hangouts for derelicts, homosexual bars, and residential streets. Another common example that might be added is the beach or strip of beach formally open to the public but pre-empted by a group of habitual users—as in the case of the "Pumphouse Gang" vividly depicted by Tom Wolfe some years ago: teenage surfbums whose jealously defended "clubhouse" was a popular section of southern California beach.

But exactly! This beach *is* verboten for people practically 50 years old. This is a segregated beach. They can look down on Windansea Beach and see nothing but lean tan kids. It is posted "no swimming" (for safety reasons), meaning surfing only. In effect, it is segregated by age.

Public beaches—like public libraries, town squares, and community playgrounds—represent public territories which tend to overlap not only home territories but also interactional territories— i.e., "any area where a social gathering may occur." In this amorphous context of brief encounters and transient huddles, "territory" is of course no longer fixed or permanent; it moves with the gathering as a kind of social membrane, to use Goffman's phrase, and vanishes when the group breaks up. Beaches also provide evidence of the operation of body territories, which Lyman and Scott describe as "the most private and inviolable of territories belonging to an individual," comprising "the space encompassed by the human body and the anatomical space of the body." Given the multidimensional territoriality of beach behavior, it is not surprising that social scientists have increasingly turned their attention to this outdoor laboratory for data on the mutations and permutations of territorial spacing.

A common purpose of beachgoers, and more especially of those who are alone, is self-presentation—the communication to others of signals designed to convey the proper impression of identity, personality, availability, and the like. An instructive fictional portrayal of such a public performance is found in a novel by William Sansom (cited by Goffman) in which an Englishman named Preedy, vacationing in Spain, makes his entrance on the beach fronting his hotel:

But in any case he took care to avoid catching anyone's eye. First of all, he had to make it clear to those potential companions of his holiday that they were of no concern to him whatsoever. He stared through them, round them, over them—eyes lost in space. The beach might have been empty. If by chance a ball was thrown his way, he looked surprised; then let a smile of amusement lighten his face (Kindly Preedy), looked round dazed to see that there *were* people on the beach, tossed it back with a smile to himself and not a smile *at* the people, and then resumed carelessly his nonchalant survey of space.

But it was time to institute a little parade, the parade of the Ideal Preedy. By devious handlings he gave any who wanted to look a chance to see the title of his book—a Spanish translation of Homer, classic thus, but not daring, cosmopolitan too—and then gathered together his beach-wrap and bag into a neat sand-resistant pile (Methodical and Sensible Preedy), rose slowly to stretch at ease his huge frame (Big-Cat Preedy), and tossed aside his sandals (Carefree Preedy, after all).[2]

As Goffman has noted in commenting on this tableau, there is often a discrepancy between impressions given deliberately and impressions "given off" unwittingly. A classic example of this in fiction is the beach episode of James Joyce's *Ulysses*, in which two strangers, Leopold Bloom and Gerty MacDowell, conduct an intense visual flirtation at a distance, aided by the shadows of fading daylight. For the virginal Gerty, the encounter is fantasized in the chaste terms of popular love stories, and her impression management is appropriately romantic; for the middle-aged and disenchanted Bloom, the episode is simply erotic—spiced by the inadvertent disclosure that the girl is lame.

Most social scientists, unlike novelists, confine their descriptions of communicative behavior to that which can be directly observed or overheard. In *People Space: The Making and Breaking of Human Boundaries*, Norman Ashcroft and Albert E. Scheflen have constructed a detailed scenario of territorial behavior on the beach that describes "people entering a scene, engaging in typical encounters, and adjusting to the arrival of newcomers." The hypothetical scene begins with the arrival of a single person, Tom, who "took off his beach robe, folded it, and placed it on the sand. He sat down, removed his sunglasses and shoes, and placed these objects and a pack of cigarettes next to the robe. Tom held the territory occupied by his body and his possessions." Shortly thereafter Tom was joined by a couple; the three then formed a conversational group, with Tom standing about a yard away from the others while they stood only a few inches apart from each other, now and then touching. From Tom's positioning and movements, plus his ruddy physical appearance, the authors deduce other personal characteristics in a manner reminiscent of Sherlock Holmes: "This behavior helped confirm that Tom was Irish-American, for people with an ancestry from the British Isles or Northern Europe use about a square yard of space when in normal conversation in uncrowded conditions."

INVASIONS OF SPACE

Students of social behavior have discovered that an effective, if indecorous, way of determining spatial boundaries and psychic tolerances is to test them directly by willfully approaching and "intruding" until signs of stress, avoidance, or flight occur. "The best way to learn the location of invisible boundaries," as Sommer has put it, "is to keep walking until somebody complains." In this connection Michael Argyle and Janet Dean have proposed an "approach-avoidance" theory of proximity which holds that persons are both attracted and repelled by others and accordingly tend to place themselves in an "equilibrium position" vis-à-vis those they encounter. "If two people like one another, according to this theory, the approach forces would be stronger and greater proximity occurs." It was found experimentally that when pairs of subjects were placed two, six, and ten feet apart, at two feet they leaned backward, while at ten feet they leaned forward—as if unconsciously seeking the proper spatial balance. Interestingly, it was also discovered that people approach closer to others whose eyes are shut—conspicuously so in the case of males approaching females who are in that state. (Not being novelists, the researchers refrained from speculating about possible motives on either side.)

In order to test the invisible boundaries of personal territory and privacy, Sommer sent his agents into the study halls of college libraries equipped with strategies and techniques of spatial invasion. The basic scenario was to violate the tacit rules of study-hall etiquette (geared to enabling students to ignore one another and maintain territorial preserves) by sitting alongside or directly across from a student at an empty or uncrowded table and sometimes closing the distance even further. Reactions to this invasion were varied but fell into identifiable patterns:

Occupying an adjacent chair and moving it closer to the subject produced the quickest departures. . . . There were also wide individual differences in the way the subjects reacted—there was no single reaction to someone sitting too close. There are defensive gestures, such as putting one's hand up to the side of the head, averting one's eyes and placing one's elbow out as a barrier against the invader, a shift in posture such as moving over half-way in one's chair, or hunching oneself over one's books, as well as attempts to move one's chair away from the invader. If these fail or are ignored by the invader, or if he shifts position too, the subject eventually takes to flight.[3]

Other investigators have devised experimental approaches and confrontations in more open settings. In a study concerned with the role of sensory stimulation in the management of space, Paul D. Nesbitt and Girard Steven posted "stimulus persons" in customer queues lined up for attractions at an amusement park. "It was found that [subjects] immediately behind them in line stood further away when the stimulus persons wore brightly colored clothes (high stimulus intensity condition) than when they wore more conservative clothing." People also stood farther away when the stimulus persons used perfume or after-shave lotion than when they used none, even when the aromatic individual was of the opposite sex (a finding that would seem to refute the claims of cosmetics boosters).

Another instance of experimental intrusion is provided by Michael Wolff in a field study of pedestrian behavior in New York City, in which the investigators conducted a series of "trial runs" on a busy sidewalk (42nd Street) in order to ascertain, among other things, when and how pedestrians yield to one another. The basic stratagem was for the experimenters to walk directly toward an approaching unaccompanied pedestrian and to appear unyielding, so as (literally) to force the issue.

The experimenters had originally determined not to give way in any circumstances, in order to avoid biasing the results, but soon found that their research was turning into a hazardous occupation. "[A] number of 'unforgivable' collisions occurred on trial runs, and the experimenters, discomfited by the victims' expressions of displeasure, changed the procedure" and veered from a collision course at the last minute or when the subject showed some sign of changing direction.

From this and other studies of what may be called approach behavior, it has become evident that there are virtually as many rules, customs, and conventions governing the conduct of "sidewalkers" as there are for car drivers, the difference being that the sidewalk rules are unwritten and tacit and (until the advent of the sociology of everyday life) completely unnoticed. Both the necessity and the intricacy of these traffic rules have been emphasized by Goffman in *Relations in Public:* "Take, for example, techniques that pedestrians employ in order to avoid bumping into one another. These seem of little significance. However, there are an appreciable number of such devices; they are *constantly* in use and they cast a pattern on street behavior. Street traffic would be a shambles without them." These common understandings control the flow of two-way traffic on either side of an invisible dividing line, the rites of passage from one "lane" to another, the traditions of civility by which one walker yields or defers to another, the degree of acceptable contact with others both physically and visually, and so on. Perhaps the most impressive aspect of this daily ritual of approach and avoidance, as Goffman has pointed out, is its demonstration of the existence of an element of *trust* between strangers, a small display of courtesy that an earlier generation would have called manners.

The ephemeral human connection established in such pedestrian encounters is, of course, as precarious as it is fragile. It is based on a kind of *laissez-faire* agreement to which Goffman has given the name "civil inattention," occurring when "one gives to another enough visual notice to demonstrate that one appreciates that the other is present (and that one admits openly to having seen him), while at the next moment withdrawing one's attention from him so as to express that he does not constitute a target of special curiosity or design." The inattention that is civilly accorded to others, in public places where strangers commingle, is not only visual but extends to the deployment of body and voice. In elevators, subways, and buses the passengers normally recognize one another's private space by standing or sitting as far apart as possible, minimizing their own movements and remaining silent—trusting that others will accord them the same respect. But this grant of trust carries the perpetual risk of being abused; while it encourages most others to reciprocate, it encourages some others to take advantage. Civil inattention may be carried too far—as when fellow passengers maintain their silence and isolation where a helpful hand or word of warning would be in order. Again, the conventional decorum dictating silence and passivity even under crowded conditions makes possible surreptitious offenses and violations that would otherwise be unlikely, ranging from pocket-picking to sexual overtures.

Some observers of the contemporary urban scene, such as the geographer David Lowenthal, have been markedly less impressed by the civil rites of deference and respect among strangers than by their opposite: the appearance of a kind of protective screen or selective perception through which only significant others are recognized or noticed while strangers are reduced to the status of nonpersons.

What environmental role do we assign to those whom we see—or sometimes bump against—without knowing as individuals or caring to place in our social network? . . . We seem to identify folk met en route as *non*-people. . . . To us they are almost members of another species. . . . We end up by divesting ourselves of responsibility for whatever happens to these non-persons even if they live in the same building: witness the Kitty Genovese affair.*[4]

What this bleak appraisal of public behavior attests to is the difficulty of maintaining norms of etiquette and civility in urban surroundings marked by congestion, stress, and anonymity, not to mention the absence of traditional neighborhood and community ties. In light of this modern condition it is not surprising that students of interpersonal space and territoriality have come to be concerned less with how the rules are kept than with how they are broken. Personal "modalities of violation," including placement of the body and hands, "penetrating" use

* Kitty Genovese was assaulted and murdered on a Queens, New York, sidewalk in full view and hearing of scores of neighbors in overlooking apartments who ignored her repeated screams for help.

of the eyes (looking and staring), noise-making, improper or impertinent address, and bodily excreta (including odor) are but the most particular of social intrusions. On a larger social scale, Ashcroft and Scheflen point out that what constitutes spatial invasion at the level of classes and groups is a relative and ever-changing matter.

Intrusion . . . is not simply a matter of physical presence in a territory, but also a question of presence at a certain time of the day, week, or year. . . . As we have seen in America and elsewhere, what constitutes an intrusion at one point in history becomes a rightful and legal pattern in another. We have yet to witness, however, the time when all citizens have been granted the same rights of privacy or the same unobscured rights to access. Intrusions are related to ideology, law, and politics.[5]

In short, one man's access is another man's excess.

DAILY APPROACHES: RITUALS AND ROUNDS

Everyone is familiar with the succession of little ceremonies involved in the daily effort to "prepare a face to meet the faces that you meet." These preparatory rites begin with the morning routines of grooming and dressing and reach a climax with the entrance on the institutional scene in which the family breaks its fast. Much may depend on the successful management of that initial appearance and first impression. For George F. Babbitt, the antihero of Sinclair Lewis's classic fable of the American middle

class, identity itself turned on the wearing of a proper set of spectacles. When he put them on, "his
head suddenly appeared not babyish but weighty,
and you noted his heavy, blunt nose, his straight
mouth and thick, long upper lip, his chin overfleshy
but strong; with respect you beheld him put on the
rest of his uniform as a Solid Citizen."[6]

Thus armed and fortified, Babbitt goes forth to
undertake his first dramatic presentation of self: that
of Autocrat of the Breakfast Table. That ritual act is
succeeded during the day by other performances in
other roles, requiring additional entrances on varying stages—each one taxing the personal resources of
organization, ingenuity, and diplomacy. Let us ac-
company Babbitt on his morning round of self-
presentations. En route to work in his car, he stops
briefly at the service station where his identity is
nicely confirmed:

The familiarity of the rite fortified him. . . . He was
flattered by the friendliness with which Sylvester Moon,
dirtiest and most skilled of motor mechanics, came out to
serve him. "Mornin', Mr. Babbitt!" said Moon, and Babbitt felt himself a person of importance, one whose name
even busy garagemen remembered—not one of these
cheap-sports flying around in flivvers.[7]

On arriving at his office building, Babbitt
negotiates a diplomatic passage through a subculture
of service and custodial personnel whose greetings
provide him with further positive reinforcement of
self.

At midday it is likely that Babbitt, and his myriad
fellow entrepeneurs, will proceed to restaurants or

coffee shops where they will participate in a rite that Goffman, in *Relations in Public*, has termed an "entrance cycle":

Just outside the entrance, the incomer may take a làst opportunity to perform a grooming check on his personal front; upon entrance, the moment that is given to taking off outside clothes, waiting for other members of the party, addressing himself to the hostess, and so on provides the cover and distance required in order to safely engage in a scanning operation.

When he is seated in the restaurant, instantly situated in the role of diner, Babbitt or his surrogate becomes a participant-observer at the performance of another professional: the waiter. The stylized approach of the skilled waiter has been often described but rarely interpreted with the insight shown by Jean-Paul Sartre:

His movement is quick and forward, a little too precise, a little too rapid. He comes toward the patrons with a step a little too quick. He bends forward a little too eagerly; his voice, his eyes express an interest a little too solicitous for the order of the customer. . . . All his behavior seems to us a game. He applies himself to chaining his movements as if they were mechanisms. . . . He is playing, he is amusing himself. But what is he playing? We need not watch long before we can explain it: he is playing at being a waiter in a café.[8]

It is essential to the role-playing of the waiter, as Sartre goes on to point out, that he stay within the limits of his prescribed part and not attempt to transcend it by disclosing irrelevant aspects of himself—such as, for example, by complaining of fatigue or exhibiting snapshots of his family. The protocols of waiter-customer relations, like those governing pedestrians and library users, are geared to the maintenance of social distance, civil inattention, and what might be termed mutual "benign neglect." Conversational small talk may be permitted, but not genuine dialogue—which would present an unacceptable and threatening demand for recognition at the close quarters of personal intimacy. Sartre continues:

This obligation is not different from that which is imposed on all tradesmen. Their condition is wholly one of ceremony. The public demands of them that they realize it as a ceremony; there is the dance of the grocer, of the tailor, of the auctioneer, by which they endeavor to persuade their clientele that they are nothing but a grocer, an auctioneer, a tailor. A grocer who dreams is offensive to the buyer, because such a grocer is not wholly a grocer. . . . There are indeed many precautions to imprison a man in what he is, as if we lived in perpetual fear that he might escape from it, that he might break away and suddenly elude his condition.[9]

But it would be a serious mistake to suppose that the formal servility of the waiter or other tradesman reflects actual subordination, let alone a state of oppression. Observers of the commercial scene have perceived what ordinary experience confirms, that in this transactional relationship it is not always (perhaps it is not often) the customer who has the upper hand. The strategic approach of the café waitress, according to W. F. Whyte in "When Workers and Customers Meet," contains an element of impression management that is calculated to secure a preliminary advantage:

The first point that stands out is that the waitress who bears up under pressure does not simply respond to her customers. She acts with some skill to control their behavior. The first question to ask when we look at the customer relationship is, "Does the waitress get the jump on the customer, or does the customer get the jump on the waitress?" The skilled waitress realizes the crucial nature of this question.

This silent struggle of the coffee shop is not an isolated phenomenon. The course of everyday life in the modern world—of "getting through the day"—might be described as a series of little stand-offs and negotiated settlements, of bargains struck, points scored, confrontations met or evaded, and embarrassments of various sorts accommodated. It says something about the anxious character of daily living that a substantial new literature has accumulated on the general subject of how to cope with these interpersonal crises—the contributions ranging from popular counsels on the arts of intimidation and self-assertion to scholarly researches into the remotest corners and shortest moments of human interaction. A particularly interesting example of the latter is the attention that has been given to the experience of embarrassment. As Goffman has noted in *Interaction Ritual*, " . . . in our Anglo-American society, at least, there seems to be no social encounter which cannot become embarrassing to one or more of its participants, giving rise to what is sometimes called an incident or false note." Doubtless there has been no lack of occasions for discomfiture and loss of face in other cultures and other periods of history; but judging from the extent of present interest and inquiry, it would almost seem that we have embarked on an Age of Embarrassment. However that may be, recent researchers have found it remarkably easy to amass evidence on the subject (what might be termed the "riches of embarrassment"). Thus Edward Gross and Gregory O. Stone, in "Embarrassment and the Analysis of Role Requirements," collected from students and others "at least one thousand specimens of embarrassment" based on personal recollections. These were then classified into a total of no less than 74 categories of *faux pas* or *gaffes*, prominent among which were the exposure of false fronts, making mistakes in public, body exposure, being caught in a cover story, being forced to choose between friends, misnaming or forgetting names, loss of visceral control, invasion of others' private (back) regions, and sudden recognition of wounds or other stigmata. In turn these categories were whittled down to three general areas of explanation: "(1) inappropriate identity; (2) loss of poise; (3) disturbance of the assumptions persons make about one another in social transactions." To these generalized sources of embarrassment Argyle has added two other probable causes: a failure of "meshing," in which roles conflict or are confused, and a breakdown of social skills in which actions normally under control go awry and lead to accidents or "snafus." A memorable illustration of the failure of motor skills is cited by Argyle in *Social Interaction:*

One of Garfinkel's examples shows how embarrassment can be multipely determined, and fall into more than one of our categories: a man at a banquet was told his zip-fastener was undone, on doing it up he caught the tablecloth in it, and on standing up to make his speech he pulled everything off the table. This could be seen as a case of discrediting of self-presentation, as failure to control equipment, as lack of social techniques to handle the situation, all of this taking place at a public and formal occasion.

Embarrassments may, of course, occur at any point of interaction whether formal or informal, intimate or casual; but it does seem that the process of approaching is fraught with a particular vulnerability. People continually "run into" one another, stumble, step on toes, miss cues, sidestep simultaneously, gesture inappropriately, say the wrong word, or make the wrong move. A common occasion of social awkwardness, noted by Goffman, is the chance encounter of fellow workers of unequal status outside the job setting where the bureaucratic conventions of distance and deference do not readily apply. "These difficulties are especially likely to occur in elevators, for there individuals who are not quite on chatting terms must remain for a time too close together to ignore the opportunity for informal talk—a problem solved, of course, for some, by special executive elevators."

The importance attached to the protocols of approach behavior by students of the sociable scene is amply confirmed by ordinary language. We are linguistically directed to get off on the right foot and to put our best foot forward—to look smart, be cool, step lively, and hold our head high. Ever attentive to first impressions, we set out on our good behavior to make an entrance with the proper approach, to fit in, maintain the right appearance, and not create a scene (though we may make the scene). The expressions that are given, and the impressions given off, in the course of all the entrance cycles and access rituals of everyday life constitute not only a role performance but a declaration of identity, a claim to recognition, and (paraphrasing Norman Mailer's title) an "advertisement for oneself."

Approaching, as we have seen, is no simple unitary act geared to an invariable objective. Nor is it, by virtue of its social character, necessarily a sociable act. It may be the stealthy tread of the human predator (mugger or burglar), fraught with hostile significance; it may be an incidental aspect of sidewalk strolling, a "rite of passage" without intentional import; it may be a magisterial entrance, accompanied by flourishes and announcements; or it may be a calculated opening gambit in an interpersonal contest (an interview, a date, a confrontation) of uncertain outcome. Approaches may be spectacular or furtive, momentous or trivial in meaning; what they share in common is their communication (voluntary or involuntary) of behavioral cues and clues, premonitory signals of the shape of things to come. A volume could be written on the varieties of approaching experience; fortunately our concern in these pages is with the ordinary rather than the extraordinary, the common and usual practices of face-to-face communication in the familiar world of everyday existence. Much of the time, in this world, approaching is the preliminary to *meeting*; accordingly it is to that regular and recurrent event—close encounters of the first kind—that we next turn our attention.

2 | MEETING: Civil Rites and Contact Rituals

This book discusses four questions: How do you say Hello? How do you say Hello back? What do you say after you say Hello? and, principally, the plaintive query, What is everybody doing instead of saying Hello?

—Eric Berne

In brief, whenever one individual runs up against another, he is likely to say hello or excuse me. . . . Moreover, as we shall also see, conversational encounters of the more extended kind are typically opened and closed by these devices, if not built up in terms of them. Surely, then, in spite of the bad name that etiquette has given to etiquette, it is time to study these performances.

—Erving Goffman

The subject of interpersonal meeting, like that of approaching, gathered a flourishing practical literature (etiquette manuals) long before it attracted any literature that could be termed theoretical. In effect, the ceremonies of contact were perceived in terms of art (and craft) before they came to be defined in terms of science. How to say hello (to peers, elders, superiors, strangers); when to touch or shake hands; whether to bow or nod, advance or retreat, genuflect or grovel—these and other questions of introductory decorum have historically been treated with elaborate seriousness by human societies. Although the terminology of manners, morals, and the finishing-school repertoire has a quaintly archaic ring to the contemporary ear, it should not be thought that these are matters of ancient history which the democratization of behavior has rendered obsolete. On the contrary, because we leave our families, divorce, move, change jobs, and join various recreational groups more rapidly today, it is probable that the rites of meeting and greeting have become more problematic, more consciously and anxiously attended to, in our own time than ever before.

Not surprisingly, initial scholarly attention to the routines of meeting and greeting came not from observers of modern society but from anthropologists in the remote fields of tribal culture. A civil rite that was all too ordinary, and hence beneath notice, in our own world became extraordinary when performed by Nanook of the North or Moana of the South Seas. In this area of human behavior, as in others, observational distance lent enchantment, while familiarity bred contempt. Although this imbalance of attention has begun to be corrected in recent years, notably by microsociologists and ethnomethodologists, the perceptibility gap remains conspicuous. For every fragment of systematic observation dealing with the hails and farewells of everyday modern life, there are archives of material devoted to the ways in which these matters are handled by distant and primitive peoples. Here, by way of illustration, is a catalogue of exotic variations in greeting behavior compiled by an anthropologist, Weston LaBarre:

Greeting kinemes vary greatly from culture to culture. In fact, many of these motor habits in one culture are open to grave misunderstanding in another. For example, the Copper Eskimo welcome strangers with a buffet on the head or shoulders with the fist, while the northwest Amazonians slap one another on the back in greeting. Polynesian men greet one another by embracing and rubbing each other's back; Spanish-American males greet one another by a stereotyped embrace, head over the right shoulder of the partner, three pats on the back, head over recriprocal left shoulder, three more pats. In the Torres Straits, the old form of greeting was to bend the right hand into a hook, then mutually scratching palms by drawing away the rigid hand, repeating this several times. An Ainu, meeting his sister, grasped her hands in his for a few seconds, suddenly released his hold, grasped her by both ears and gave the peculiar Ainu greeting cry; then they stroked one another down the face and shoulders. Kayan males in Borneo grasp each other by the forearm, while a host throws his arm over the shoulder of a guest and strokes him endearingly with the palm of his hand. When two Kurd males meet, they grasp one another's right hand, raise them both, and alternately kiss the other's hand. Andamanese greet one another by one sitting down in the lap of the other, arms around each other's necks and weeping for a while; two brothers, father and son, mother and daughter, and husband and wife, or even two friends may do this; the husband sits in the lap of the wife. Friends' "goodbye" consists in raising the hand of the other to the mouth and gently blowing on it, reciprocally. At Matavai a full-dress greeting after long absence requires scratching the head and temples with a shark's tooth, violently and with much bleeding. This brief list could be easily enlarged by other anthropologists.[1]

THE BOW: MEETINGS EAST AND WEST

Not only do the formalities of greeting vary widely between cultures; they also vary within cultures, especially those that are undergoing rapid change. Generally the old ways are more formal, elaborate, and stylized, often requiring special training and considerable dexterity; they reflect the hierarchical structure of traditional society, with its sensitivity to gradations of age, rank, and station. A Japanese guidebook observes:

In the past it was the proper etiquette in Japan, on meeting a senior who was on foot while one was riding in a vehicle, to alight from the vehicle and make a bow. Also it has been the custom when meeting on the street to take off coats and scarves before extending greetings. This may still be seen done on the streets of even such modern cities as Tokyo, but in the present age our new etiquette does not require it. The only point that must be remembered is that when meeting a senior on the street one must always be sure to stop first and then bow. If one arm is occupied, the other, even singly, should be drawn palm-down properly to the knees.[2]

In Japan the bow is the essential kineme for social interaction of all kinds. "It is the way we greet our friends, pay respect to each other, express thanks, apologize, ask favors of each other, and say goodbye." A scholarly Japanese observer defines its value succinctly: "Bowing is the beginning of human relations." Apart from individual nuances and embellishments, stylized bowing in Japan is divided into three stages or degrees: the deep bow of obeisance (*saikeirei*), formerly addressed only to the Emperor and now considered obsolete; the ordinary salutation (with approximately 30-degree bending of the body), and the light bow (15-degree bend). In an exchange of bows between persons of different rank, the social inferior makes the deeper as well as the final bow. Formerly it was customary in Japan to bow not only on greeting but repeatedly, after every few words of conversation; nowadays this practice is considered too strenuous and has been modified to a few light bows. But there is still opportunity for confusion and even for competition. "Frequently one tries to be the more polite one, and this can result in a 'bowing contest' which Wagatsuma calls 'one-downmanship.' " The onus is very much on the social inferior, who must often change his own course or even retreat in the face of an oncoming superior. For example, as a Western observer noted, "On meeting one's seniors in a narrow hallway one should pause at the left, bow slightly, and await the other's passage. If starting up a stairway, one should return to the bottom and there await the passage of the other person. At all other times one goes to the left and waits."

In Western nations, and particularly in Germany, the act of bowing is still commonly practiced as an expression of respect, but in America it has come more and more to be reserved for ceremonial or mock-ceremonial occasions and for public performances where actors may "take a bow" without appearing excessively formal. Some American etiquette books still counsel a light bow for men and boys on being introduced to the opposite sex; but for most Americans, lacking a feudal tradition or an ingrained acceptance of class distinctions, bowing has long been regarded as a somewhat effete and somehow submissive act inconsistent with the egalitarian ethos. Where it is still observed at all, the depth of the bow has been so drastically reduced that it is often little more than a nod of the head. The elements of deference and formality have been preserved intact in the military salute; but among civilian Americans the clear successor to the bow is the more informal and intimate gesture of the handshake.

THE HANDSHAKE

The origin of the handshake is obscure, and its significance has been variously interpreted. An interesting, if anthropologically unsound, theory is that of Ortega y Gasset, who has perceived in the gesture the submission of the vanquished to the victor or of the slave to his master. More plausible is the common view that the handshake was (and is) a signal of friendly or peaceable intentions, the presentation of an open hand conveying the absence of a weapon. Whatever its historical origins, the handshake is clearly a tactile communication, not unrelated to such other contact rituals as the "laying on of hands," the placing together of the palms of the hands, placing a hand on the other's heart, nose rubbing, embracing, kissing, backslapping, and the like. Edward Westermarck long ago recognized that these diverse forms of salutation by contact "are obviously direct expressions of affection." He added that

. . . we can hardly doubt that the joining of hands serves a similar object when we find it combined with other tokens of good will. Among some of the Australian natives, friends, on meeting after an absence, "will kiss, shake hands, and sometimes cry over one another." In Morocco equals salute each other by joining their hands with a quick motion, separating them immediately; and kissing each his own hand. The Soolimas, again, place the palms of the right hands together, carry them to the forehead, and from thence to the left side of the chest.[3]

Among the many variations in handshaking behavior, there are noteworthy sexual differences. In Europe and America it is customary for men to shake hands with each other but less common for women to do so; they tend to kiss or embrace when they meet friends and are likely to shake hands only when meeting for the first time or as casual acquaintances. Normally men do not shake hands with women (here the bow is still in effect) unless the woman first extends her hand, when in the English-speaking world it will be shaken and in the Latin-speaking world it will be kissed. The male-male (*mano a mano*) handshake varies along subcultural lines, often signaling membership in a particular group or association. Some American lodges and clubs have devised distinctive and arcane handclasps; the youth counterculture of the 1960s developed a "thumbshake" conveying the peace sign (but reverted to the conventional handshake to greet elders or squares); and black youths have substituted a form of handslapping in encounters with peers. Differences of class as well as of personality are evident in the humorous description of British practices by the nineteenth-century wit Sidney Smith.

Have you noticed how people shake your hand? There is the *high-official*—the body erect, and a rapid, short shake, near the chin. There is the *mortmain*—the flat hand introduced into your palm, and hardly conscious of its contiguity. The *digital*—one finger held out, much used by the high clergy. There is the *shakus rusticus*, where your hand is seized in an iron grasp, betokening rude health, warm heart, and distance from the Metropolis; but producing a strong sense of relief on your part when you find your hand released and your fingers unbroken. The next to this is the *retentive shake*—one which, beginning with vigour, pauses as it were to take breath, but without relinquishing its prey, and before you are aware begins again, till you feel anxious as to the result, and have no shake left in you. Worse, there is the *pisces*—the damp palm like a dead fish, equally silent, equally clammy, and leaving its odour in your hand.

Written in 1820, Smith's commentary barely avoids refuting the recent contention of Desmond Morris that the handshake "did not gain wide usage until almost a hundred and fifty years ago." But it is likely that, as Morris argues, the custom became widespread as a result of the rise of the middle classes following the Industrial Revolution; the handshake was a convenient way of sealing a commercial bargain by "giving one's hand on it." Even this gesture, however, was practiced in antiquity; among the Romans a pledge of honor, if not of profit, was commonly sealed with a handclasp. Closely following Plutarch, Shakespeare gave the conspiratorial Brutus the line "Give me your hands all over, one by one." And the grasping, if not the clasping, of hands—as well as of wrists, arms, and shoulders—as a gesture of conviviality or communion appears so often in so many and diverse cultures as to suggest a spontaneous act expressive not merely of cultural peculiarities but of a universal human connection.

The significance attached to the handshake in Western societies, and particularly in America, as a token of personal friendliness and trust is exemplified by the time-honored rite of mass handshaking to which politicians, willingly or unwillingly, are required to conform. Among the more willing was President Calvin Coolidge, a notoriously nonverbal personality, who opened the White House to the public every day and claimed that "on one occasion I shook hands with 1,900 in 34 minutes." Even more efficient was President Theodore Roosevelt, who is reported to have shaken 8,513 hands on one memorable New Year's Day. President Lyndon Johnson, a singularly tactile communicator, was an enthusiastic devotee of "pressing the flesh" and would seize as many as four or five outstretched hands at one time. For the political candidate this digital contact is the purest form of public relations, symbolizing that he has his hand on the pulse of the public and is in touch with the grass roots; but the initiative in such ceremonial encounters more often comes from the side of the public than from that of the personage involved. "There is something about shaking the hand of a candidate," according to Theodore White, "that gives people the feeling they are wired in to history, a part of it all."

Professional counselors in the sociable arts of winning friends and influencing people have emphasized the positive value of a firm clasp and the negative significance of a limp or weak handshake. The worst impression of all, according to one such authority, is conveyed by the refusal to shake hands: "I believe that, excluding verbal or physical attack, the most rejecting insult one individual can offer another is to refuse to shake an outstretched hand. It is equivalent to spitting on someone."

On the other hand, the strategic offering or withholding of the handshake as a therapeutic device has been recommended by the late founder of Transactional Analysis, Eric Berne, whose book *What Do You Say After You Say Hello?* describes his own strategy with patients in psychologically detailed terms:

Many patients who come to a psychiatrist for the first time introduce themselves and shake hands when he invites them into his office. Some psychiatrists, indeed, offer their hands first. I have a different policy in regard to handshakes. If the patient proffers his hand in a hearty way, I will shake it in order to avoid being rude, but in a noncommittal fashion, because I am wondering why he is being so hearty. . . . If he proffers it in a way which indicates that he is desperate, then I will shake it firmly and reassuringly to let him know that I understand his need. But my manner when I enter the waiting room, the expression on my face and the position of my arms, indicates clearly enough to most newcomers that this amenity will be omitted unless they insist upon it. . . . Mainly, I do not shake hands with them because I do not know them, and I do not expect them to shake hands with me, because they do not know me; also, some people who come to psychiatrists object to being touched, and it is a courtesy to them to refrain from doing so.

However, at the conclusion of the interview, Berne would generally make a point of shaking hands with the patient to indicate acceptance and reassurance, with one categorical exception: "On the other side, if he has lied to me out of malice rather than natural embarrassment, or tried to exploit or browbeat me, I will not shake hands with him, so that he knows he will have to behave differently if he wants me on his side."

GREETINGS AND SALUTATIONS

Meetings of every sort—whether accidental, casual, or fraught with expectation—call forth appropriate displays of greeting behavior. Although these performances vary widely in their details among cultures and subcultures, there are some elementary moves common to most societies. Irenaeus Eibl-Eibesfeldt and his co-workers claimed to find a shared pattern of expression and gesture associated with "distance greetings" in such differing environments as Europe, Bali, Samoa, New Guinea, and Brazil (where the pattern was filmed), as well as in Africa, Japan, Hong Kong, and Peru (where it was observed):

Unless there is hostility, a greeting will take place when two people have approached each other closely enough to recognize each other's facial expressions, or being already close, establish visual contact for the first time. The greeting pattern consists of a smile, followed by a rapid raising of the eyebrows, which stay raised for approximately one sixth of a second. Finally, there is a nodding of the head, with the smile continuing.

On many occasions, the greeting ritual is likely to be both more extensive and more intensive, as indicated by Goffman's analysis of the usual situation:

Two individuals upon approaching orient frontally to each other. Their glances lock for a moment in communion, eyes glisten, smiling expressions of social recognition are conveyed, and a note of pleasure is briefly sustained. Hand-waving, hat-tipping, and other "appeasement gestures" may be performed. A verbal salutation is likely to be provided along with a term of address. When possible, embracing, handshaking, and other bodily contacting may occur.[4]

A common element in first meetings, when the parties are not well known to each other, is *caution*; overtures are restrained and often formal, verbal greetings are standardized and uninformative, self-disclosure is tentative and guarded. In *Games People Play*, Berne has set down the typically laconic form of what he calls the "American greeting ritual":

"Hi!" (Hello, good morning.)
"Hi" (Hello, good morning.)
"Warm enough forya?" (How are you?)
"Sure is. Looks like rain, though." (Fine, how are you?)
"Well, take cara yourself." (Okay.)
"I'll be seeing you."
"So long."
"So long."

This standard exchange is characterized by Berne as an "eight-stroke ritual," one that is appropriate between casual acquaintances who are not seriously interested either in the state of each other's health or in pursuing the relationship further; on the other hand, each is adequately "stroked" and the little ceremony is successfully carried through. However, if either partner fails to deliver (or exceeds) the conventional allotment of strokes, the ritual is violated and the relationship strained.

Despite the apparently perfunctory nature of this greeting ritual, important nonverbal messages are exchanged, various impressions are given off and received, and potentially serious matters are negotiated. One such matter, stressed by George J. McCall and J. L. Simmons, is the issue of *identity*— both of oneself and of the other:

In their first encounter, unacquainted people face the problem of identification in its purest and most agonizing form. Who is the other person? Who am I in this situation? Who *could* I be? What do I *want* to be? Who does *he* want me to be? . . . Each party must read the person with extra care for any clues to identity that he may give or give off.[5]

In addition to reading the other person, each party to the transaction must decide on an appropriate social self or identity to be presented—one that will be "safe" in the circumstances and yet venturesome. According to McCall and Simmons, "Each must cautiously, very tentatively and subtly, hint at some of the less commonplace aspects of his identities while anchoring his performance on his 'safe' identities—a distinction that is only relative, to be sure."

It would seem that first meetings, more than other social interactions, are characterized by what Albert K. Cohen has called exploratory gestures. "By a casual, semi-serious, non-committal or tangential remark I may stick my neck out just a little way, but I will quickly withdraw it unless you, by some sign of affirmation, stick *yours* out." This reciprocal exchange of approval or acceptance serves not only the social purpose of advancing a relationship but also the psychological need of verifying to oneself the provisional identity that is being tried on and tried out. Following the classic formulation of the social "looking-glass self" originally proposed by Cooley at the turn of the century, Cohen maintains in effect that identity, like beauty, is in the eye of the beholder. "The important thing to remember is that we do not first convert ourselves and then others. The acceptability (of claiming an identity) to oneself depends upon its acceptability to others. Converting the other is part of the process of converting oneself."

Prior to this process of mutual conversion and confirmation, in meetings of the everyday kind, there is a preparatory stage involving what may be termed threshold tactics—that is, premonitory signals or announcements of arrival such as knocking on the door, clearing one's throat, or verbally hailing the other. These preliminary gestures are, in Goffman's term, "the first mover's first move," falling within the traditions of civility and courtesy which serve to protect privacy, avoid intrusion, and minimize the element of surprise. The word "hello," as Goffman points out, may itself function not as a greeting but as a summons to the recipient indicating that a contact or audience is being sought; it may also represent a polite warning to unseen others that someone is about to enter their territory.

In the arts of sociability, as in the arts of design, form follows function. The form of the greeting varies according to the function of the meeting. Berne, in his psychological analysis of transactions, has attempted to quantify the "strokes" exchanged in greeting rituals, on a scale ranging from two strokes (Hi-Hi) for the most casual meetings, through the eight-stroke ritual for nonintimates mentioned above, to the sustained and strenuous interaction exhibited on such occasions as reunions (up to 60 strokes).

Goffman has proposed a set of qualitative distinctions on the scale of greeting behavior moving upward from the modest "maintenance rituals" involved in "passing greetings" and "greetings of surprise," on the part of acquaintances merely acknowledging their relationship, to the more complex salutations extended by individuals about to enter into a sustained encounter (such as a dialogue, a date, or a deal). In this interpretation the brief passing greeting has only a *retrospective* character, related to past acquaintance, while the initial ritual of a genuine encounter possesses a *prospective* dimension as well:

The [passing greeting], as it were, looks in only one direction: back from the contact to the relationship of the individuals who have momentarily come into each other's ken. The greeting associated with encounters, however, looks in two directions: back to the relationship of the participants but also forward to the temporary period of increased access that has just now come into being.[6]

Meeting, then, when it is more than accidental or transient—more than of passing interest—is the prologue to occasions of heightened access and sustained interaction. After the handshakes and hellos, after the overtures and obeisances, the main event may begin—whether it be the transaction of business, the negotiation of an interview, the game of dating, or the dance of courtship. Every form of interaction has its distinctive set of codes, customs, and conventions—a ritualized character imposed by culture, refined over time, and learned anew by each generation through processes (largely unconscious) of imitation, repetition, and reinforcement. In all of the circumstances in which people approach, meet, and interact with one another there are some elements that are unique and unrepeatable, born of the moment, and other elements that are patterned and predictable. It is with the latter—the patterns of culture, the rituals of commingling, the rites of spring—that we are mainly concerned. The first two chapters have dealt, all too partially and selectively, with the common preliminaries of interaction. In the following chapter we shall explore in some detail the powerfully expressive languages of silence—the channels of nonverbal communication—through which, every day and all day, each of us continuously and eloquently holds conversation with the world.

3 | SIGNALING: Visual Cues and Mute Appeals

There's language in her eye, her cheek, her lip.

—William Shakespeare, Troilus and Cressida

But when a girl is feminine. . . *she is feminine from the top of her head to the tips of her toes. Her smile is sweet and warm, her build is usually doll-size, and she loves fussy clothes.*

—Taffy's Tips to Teens

Why, then, do you walk as if you had swallowed a ramrod?

—*Epictetus*

Demeanor [in old Japan] was most elaborately and mercilessly regulated, not merely as to obeisances, of which there were countless grades, varying according to sex as well as class—but even in regard to facial expression, the manner of smiling, the conduct of the breath, the way of sitting, standing, walking, rising. Everybody was trained from infancy in this etiquette of expression and deportment. . . .

—*Lafcadio Hearn*

In all known human societies there have been prescriptions and proscriptions governing the repertoire of what Lafcadio Hearn designated as expression and deportment. In most cultures elaborate codes of etiquette, dramatized by equally complicated rituals, have represented the primary means of educating new generations in the proper ways of walking, talking, not talking, gesturing, sitting, standing, staring, not staring, dressing, undressing, smiling, scowling, primping, preening, and so on. With the exception of talk these are the constituent elements of the "silent language"—the domain of nonverbal communication. An early and comprehensive classification of its major forms, possibly still the most useful we have, was undertaken by Jurgen Ruesch and Wendell Kees in their classic work *Nonverbal Communication: Notes on the Visual Perception of Human Relations:*

Sign Language includes all those forms of codification in which words, numbers, and punctuation signs have been supplanted by gestures; these vary from the "monosyllabic" gesture of the hitchhiker to such complete systems as the language of the deaf.

Action Language embraces all movements that are not used exclusively as signals. Such acts as walking and drinking, for example, have a dual function: on one hand they serve personal needs, and on the other they constitute statements to those who may perceive them.

Object Language comprises all intentional and nonintentional display of material things, such as implements, machines, art objects, architectural structures, and—last but not least—the human body and whatever clothes or covers it. The embodiment of letters as they occur in books and on signs has a material substance, and this aspect of words also has to be considered as object language.

BODY POLITICS: KINESIC BEHAVIOR

Just as Edward T. Hall is by common acknowledgment the conceptual father of *proxemics*, the study of spatial behavior, so Ray L. Birdwhistell is recognized as the chief innovator of *kinesics*, the discipline concerned with communicative body motion. No less important than Birdwhistell's experimental research in this field has been his imaginative, not to say liberating, approach to the total process of human communication. Before the appearance of Birdwhistell's *Introduction to Kinesics*, in 1952, it was customary to regard communication predominantly in linguistic terms, as the transmission and reception of verbal messages. In effect the study of communication was limited to a single sensory channel, the audio-acoustic or vocal; other channels, where they were acknowledged at all, were generally dismissed as "noise" or dysfunctional interference to be eliminated as much as possible—or at best as inferior adjuncts of speech ("grunts and groans"). It is the achievement of Birdwhistell and his coworkers to have relegated this obsolete unidimensional model to the scrapyard of scientific relics and to have replaced it with a multichannel model which portrays communication as a continuous process making use of all the sensory modalities—not just the auditory-acoustic channel but also a kinesthetic-visual channel, an "odor-producing olfactory" channel, a tactile channel, and so on. Communication comes to be seen as the process of orchestrating and alternating channels; "thus, while no single channel is in constant use, one or more channels are always in operation."

As the audio-acoustic channel provides the subject matter of linguistics—i.e., language and paralanguage—so the kinesthetic-visual channel supplies the data of kinesics—i.e., "body language." Before turning to the specific findings of the kinesicists, however, it is important to recognize that the activity which flows through this channel represents only part of a larger whole—the total continuous process of human communication—and cannot be understood or evaluated apart from that context. Still less so, as Birdwhistell and Hall have been at pains to point out, can a single kineme of posture or gesture be used as the basis for a judgment of personality or purpose. There may be a sense in which, as the old song declares, "every little movement has a meaning of its own," but that meaning is not in the movement but in the mover—which is to say in his nature, his culture, his immediate situation, and the intentional course of his ongoing career through the world. "I must emphasize," writes Birdwhistell in italics, "that *no position, expression, or movement ever carries meaning in and of itself.*" And Hall, in the face of a sharp increase of interest in the strategic and manipulative uses of body language, makes the cautionary point even more forcefully:

Recently, there has been a spate of books about nonverbal communication; it's fashionable and everybody's doing it. Opportunistic writers who collect samples and examples from the experts, exploiting the timeliness of the subject, only manage to describe part of the picture, and a distorted part at that. . . . When the whole process was unconscious, nobody was seen as having an advantage. Those who are fearful feel that their own behavior may be used against them and that NVC [nonverbal communication] insights have put a tool in the hands of people who want to manipulate them. . . .

Far from being a superficial form of communication that can be consciously manipulated, NVC systems are interwoven with the fabric of the personality and into society itself, even rooted in how one experiences oneself as a man or a woman. Without these unwritten systems for managing the tremendous diversity of encounters in everyday life, man would be nothing but a machine.[1]

APPEARANCES: PHYSICAL AND SARTORIAL

It will come as no surprise to media buffs—continuously exposed to the seductions of commercials and advertisements, centerfolds and sitcom heroines—to learn that physical attractiveness attracts. In this gradient of behavior and communication, the evidence of the laboratory confirms that of ordinary experience—not that "likes attract" but that the attractive are liked. Studies have consistently shown, among other things, that physical attractiveness is the most important predictor of dating invitations and solicitations, for males and females alike; that attractive females can influence male attitudes more easily than can the unattractive; that attractive female students are more successful in the strategic manipulation of teacher attitudes; that attractive persons of either sex tend to rank higher on credibility scales; and that (still no surprises) physical attractiveness is a key factor, if not the overriding one, in marriage and courtship decisions.

The major components of physical attractiveness—as attested by innumerable respondents to questionnaires and interviews—are physique, clothes, face, hair, and hands. The extent to which all of these elements are culturally conditioned may be illustrated by reference to norms governing physique or body shape. In traditional Polynesian cultures, such as the Samoan and Hawaiian, the feminine ideal (as embodied in women of the ruling caste) found expression in a degree of stature and girth commonly ranging from 200 to 300 pounds. In contemporary America, on the other hand, despite rapid fluctuations of fashion, the norm of feminine beauty as presented by magazines and pursued by compulsive dieters appears to approach the opposite extreme of skeletal thinness bordering on a clinical state of malnutrition. One of Taffy's Tips to Teens holds that "It's hard to picture a girl of large build being quite feminine, yet many chubby girls have some very pleasing feminine qualities."

One familiar method of enhancing physical attractiveness, practiced alike in mesa and metropolis, is that of body adornment—in the form of clothing, jewelry, makeup, wigs, or other artifacts. The adage that clothes make the man, and more especially the woman, expresses the common view that clothing preferences and habits are an outward index of inner character, as well as of class and calling. This was the confident view of no less an authority than Sherlock Holmes:

By a man's fingernails, by his coat-sleeve, by his boots, by his trouser-knees, by the callosities of his forefinger and thumb, by his expression, by his shirt-cuffs—by each of these things a man's calling is plainly revealed. That all united should fail to enlighten the competent inquirer in any case is almost inconceivable.

The expressive-communicative functions of dress have, of course, long been recognized and remarked on; but cultural attitudes toward its display possibilities have varied from Polonius' expansive "costly thy raiment as thy purse can buy" to the minimal advice of Lord Lyttelton as recorded by Lady Mary Wortley Montagu:

> Be plain in dress, and sober in your diet;
> In short, my deary, kiss me and be quiet.

It is likely, however, that most males with osculation on their minds would prefer the sentiment expressed by a better poet, Robert Herrick:

> A sweet disorder in the dress
> Kindles in clothes a wantonness.

The symbolic functions of clothing are not only varied but ambiguous: It may serve to conceal or reveal, to express personality or to suppress it. As Mark L. Knapp points out in *Nonverbal Communication in Human Interaction*, "To understand the relationship between clothes and communication, we should be familiar with the various functions clothes may fulfill: decoration, protection (both physical and psychological), sexual attraction, self-denial, concealment, group identification, and display of status or role." The function of role and group identification is represented most explicitly by the standardized uniform, as worn by soldiers, nurses, nuns, cops, clowns, Klansmen, and clergymen; in more subtle ways the relationship of dress to role may be so delicate that a role-player feels incompetent to perform except when properly attired. Thus the psychological dilemma of a middle-class American woman of the mid-nineteenth century. On the one hand her wardrobe contained

> Dresses for breakfasts, and dinners, and balls;
> Dresses to sit in, and stand in, and walk in;
> Dresses to dance in, and flirt in, and talk in;
> Dresses in which to do nothing at all;
> Dresses for Winter, Spring, Summer, and Fall.[2]

On the other hand:

> This same Miss McFlimsey of Madison Square,
> The last time we met was in utter despair,
> Because she had nothing whatever to wear![3]

The importance of clothing as an indicator of rank or status is especially acute in societies governed by hierarchical class structures and differential codes of conduct, such as traditional Japan. As Donald Richie observes:

Japan is one of the last countries to wear costumes. Not only the fireman and the policeman, but also the student and the laborer. There is a suit for hiking, a costume for striking; there is the unmistakable fashion for the boy who belongs to a gang and the indubitable ensemble of the fallen woman.[4]

In societies less meticulously stratified and graded, such as the American, variations in costume or clothing style may be equally numerous but are likely more often to be adopted consciously as a means of expression or presentation rather than formally imposed by tradition. For members of minority groups, as well as of deviant subcultures and "alternative lifestyles," clothes may advertise a variety of affiliations and commitments: sexual as well as occupational, political as well as ethnic. For example, American youths of the middle class frequently "dress down" (in faded jeans and thrift-shop castoffs) to demonstrate their antimaterialist ideology, while ghetto youths commonly "dress up" to disguise their economic status and perhaps, as one study indicates, to compensate for feelings of social inferiority. A study of college students during the late 1960s concluded that clothing served as a badge of political and social ideology and that the very visibility of political sympathies both facilitated the forming of like-minded groups and sharpened the cleavages between them.

POSTURES AND IMPOSTURES

Posture refers to the ways in which people stand, sit, stoop, squat, kneel, recline, and otherwise arrange their bodies. Each of these positions in turn can be analyzed in terms of what Albert E. Scheflen has called "points" and Birdwhistell labels "kines"—i.e., micro-movements or expressions which together add up to the gestalt of posture or gesture. Long before Birdwhistell initiated the scientific analysis of body-motion communication, its significance was generally if vaguely recognized and its special language intuitively understood. The state of the study in the early twentieth century was nicely summarized by the pioneer linguistic anthropologist Edward Sapir: ". . . we respond to gestures with an extreme alertness and, one might almost say, in accordance with an elaborate and secret code that is written nowhere, known by none, and understood by all."

Although there are said to be more than 1,000 different steady postures available to a human being, the number likely to be adopted by any individual is drastically reduced by constraints of culture, personality, and situational context. How (or whether) one sits, for example, is largely predetermined by cultural factors such as the form of seating (chair, ground, or tuffet), the relative rank or status of others present, the ceremonial character of the occasion (e.g., a church service or rendering of the national anthem), and so on. The function of status in this regard has been illustrated by Goffman in an account of staff meetings at a psychiatric institution, where the senior professionals occupied the front seats and adopted relaxed postures, sitting slumped in their chairs with their feet on the tables, whereas junior staff members sat farther back and in upright postures. For the most part such role-enactment is unconsciously produced and only tacitly perceived; but in strained situations or where knowledge is insecure it may be attended by conscious, and even self-conscious, awareness. An American etiquette guide addressed to teenagers indicates how complex the ground rules can be in even so elementary a maneuver as taking a chair:

A young lady never throws herself, bounces or flounces into a chair and, once there, she does not lounge in it or flop in it on the end of her spine.

The proper way is to approach the chair at an angle and pause almost in profile in front of it, with the left leg nearest the chair. As you turn, the back of your leg should touch the center front of the seat. Now make sure that your right foot is slightly ahead of the left and that your weight is on the balls of both feet. Then, using the body control your exercises should have developed (those knee bends, for instance), slowly lower your body to the seat.

As soon as you're *there*, draw your legs back and pull the right heel into the left instep, knees together. Or, as you draw your legs back, swing them slightly to one side and hook one foot around the ankle of the other. This position is especially comfortable if you are wearing a short or narrow skirt. Now arrange your hands nicely. An easy pose is to cross your hands in your lap, palms up. This will keep you from clutching your hands or twisting them or a ring on your finger, in case you're nervous—but why should you be? You look so nice and ladylike sitting there. Relax and enjoy yourself.[5]

An equivalent example from a Japanese etiquette manual suggests that floor-sitting is not necessarily (as it tends to be in American gatherings) more informal than chair-sitting:

In lowering oneself to the *tatami* [mat] for sitting, the toes of one foot are drawn back or brought forward slightly, the knees bent quietly and placed in turn on the floor. At this time the body should not lean forward. In the correct sitting posture the big toes are placed one on top of the other beneath the body. A man's knees are placed about three or four inches apart, a woman's close together; then with the body up straight, one looks toward the front. The man's hands are placed on the thigh, the woman's clasped lightly in front. When in foreign clothes it is permissible for men to sit with their legs crossed after asking permission and for women to relax the knees a little by pointing the feet out sideways. But such easy postures must never be used when in Japanese clothes or in front of a person of high position.[6]

Posture is especially noticed in relation to the act of walking—not only because movement is conspicuous but because walking, like dancing, provides obvious opportunities for the performance of roles. As Hall has noted: "Another nonverbal system is the way people walk, which communicates status, mood, gender, age, state of health, and ethnic affiliation." A graphic example of such communication has been cited by Michael Argyle:

In a street market I watched a working class mum and her daughter. The mother waddled as if her feet were playing her up. Outside a Knightsbridge hotel I watched an upper class mum and her daughter come out from a wedding reception and walk towards Hyde Park Corner, the mother on very thin legs slightly bowed as though she had wet herself. She controlled her body as if it might snap if moved too impulsively. Both daughters walked identically.

The act of walking, seemingly a simple means of locomotion, has been invested by humankind with a richness and complexity of symbolism surpassing most other activities—although scholars (in their armchairs) have been slow to perceive its significance. Like standing, it conveys the image of an "upright," as opposed to a supine, act (walking tall, walking like a man); added to this is the sense of volitional movement, of physical and personal independence. ("What do you suppose will satisfy the soul," sang Whitman, "except to walk free and own no superior?") There is often a note of estrangement and loss, as well as of pride, in the countless variations in song and story on the theme of walking alone—as in the declaration of Obadiah Milton Conover:

> Alone I walk the peopled city,
>   Where each seems happy with his own;
> O friends, I ask not for your pity—
>   I walk alone.[7]

The connotations of walking include an element of grace and dignity—as in Byron's line "He hoped now to walk softly all his days in soberness of spirit" and in Theodore Roosevelt's less felicitous "Walk softly—and carry a big stick." And in contrast to the solitary conception of the act, walking is not infrequently portrayed as a companionate and sociable behavior: "I'd rather one should walk with me," wrote Edgar Guest, "than merely tell the way." A poet of equal stature, Walter J. Graham, struck this theme heavily:

I think, when I read of the poet's desire,
That a house by the side of the road would be good;
But service is found in its tenderest form
When we walk with the crowd in the road.[8]

Extending the theme of companionship associated with walking is the Biblical message of divine support and guidance for the one who walks humbly with his God (Micah VI:8). Thus spake Isaiah (XL:31): "They that wait upon the Lord shall renew their strength; . . . they shall run, and not be weary; and they shall walk, and not faint." And Jeremiah (VI:16): "Stand ye in the ways, and see, and ask for the old paths, where is the good way, and walk therein." A typical modern version of this storied theme is found in the Rodgers and Hammerstein lyric from *Carousel:* "Walk on, walk on, with hope in your heart, and you'll never walk alone."

Doubtless the most widely observed, and thoroughly appraised, aspect of nonverbal communication conveyed by walking is that of "gender display" (to use the circumspect terminology of kinesics). Although this activity is carried out by both males and females, attention has been largely concentrated (as Goffman has noted in connection with walking) on "the half of our population whose appearance is, and is designed to be, appreciated by all and savored by some." For that very reason, in the case of a self-conscious female, exhibition may turn into inhibition:

A young woman is walking down a city street. She is excruciatingly aware of her appearance and of the reaction to it (imagined or real) of every person she meets. She walks through a group of construction workers who are eating lunch in a line along the pavement. Her stomach tightens with terror and revulsion; her face becomes contorted into a grimace of self-control and fake unawareness; her walk and carriage become stiff and dehumanized.[9]

But under happier circumstances, according to the testimony of expert witnesses, "She is pretty to walk with" (Sir John Suckling); "She walks in beauty like the night/Of cloudless climes and starry skies" (Byron); she is admired "For her gait, if she be walking" (William Browne); and there is "Something in the way she moves" that attracts Beatle George Harrison like no other lover.

In an analysis of what he calls the "black walk," Kenneth R. Johnson describes the ambulation of young black males as combining a statement about their identity as a racial minority with a stylized form of gender display intended to attract female attention. "Observing young black males walking down ghetto streets, one can't help noticing that they are, indeed, in Thoreau's words, 'marching to the tune of a different drummer.'" Whereas young white males walk briskly on the balls of their feet, with both arms swinging and a stride of assumed authority,

The young black male's walk is different. First of all, it's much slower—it's more of a stroll. The head is sometimes slightly elevated and casually tipped to the side. Only one arm swings at the side with the hand slightly cupped. The other arm hangs limply to the side or it is tucked in the pocket. The gait is slow, casual and rhythmic. The gait is almost like a walking dance, with all parts of the body in rhythmic harmony. This walk is called a "pimp strut," or it is referred to as "walking that walk."[10]

The black walk conveys a number of nonverbal messages: that the walker is beautiful, that he is sexual, and that he is "cool"—i.e., "he is not upset or bothered by the cares of the world and is, in fact, somewhat disdainful and insolent toward the world." A salient point about the black walk is that it is primarily a performance rather than a functional act of locomotion. "Sometimes," as Johnson writes, "one gets the feeling that *where* the young black male is going is not as important as *how* he gets there. There is a great deal of 'styling' in the walk. The means are more important than the end."

COURTSHIP: THE SIGNALS OF SEX

The black walk is also carried over into what Johnson calls the "rapping stance"—the posture adopted by a young black male when talking to a young black female, particularly when making the first moves that prefigure a romantic relationship.

The "rapping stance" is as follows: first, the black male does not stand directly in front of the black female but at a slight angle; the head is slightly elevated and tipped to the side (toward the female); the eyes are about three-fourths open; sometimes, the head very slowly nods as the "rap" is delivered; the arms conform to the "pimp strut" pattern—one hand may be halfway in the pocket, while the other arm hangs free; finally, the weight of the body is concentrated on the back heel (in the "rapping stance" the feet are not together but are positioned in a kind of frozen step). The black female will listen to this "rap" nonchalantly, with one hand on her hip.

This distinctive ethnic style is contrasted to the conventional behavior of the young white male in a similar heterosexual "rap"; in this case, according to Johnson, the female is backed against the wall while the male extends one arm and places his palm against the wall, leaning toward the woman with his weight on the foot closest to her. Occasionally the white male extends both arms so that the female is enclosed between them.

As the key terms in use by kinesicists suggest— courtship behavior, preening, gender display, and the like—the study of signals between the sexes has been greatly influenced by the earlier work of zoologists and ethologists in mapping the elaborate systems of regulation governing courtship and mating behavior among animal species. Birdwhistell in particular has closely followed biological precedent in his attempts at the precise description and analysis of such actions as gender identification signals. For example, he has determined that male-female differences in intrafemoral angle and arm-body angle can be measured exactly. His observations indicate that American females, when transmitting gender signals or responding to similar signals from males, "bring the legs together, at times to the point that the upper legs cross, either in a full leg cross *with feet still to-*

gether, the lateral aspects of the two feet parallel to each other, or in standing knee over knee"—in contrast to the American male position in which the intrafemoral index ranges up to an angle of 10 or 15 degrees. Comparable differences have been observed between the sexes with respect to such features as arm position and body movement. In gender presentation the American female holds her arms close to the trunk, while the male moves his arms some 5 to 10 degrees away from the body; and, in movement, the female tends to present "the entire body from neck to ankles as a moving whole," while the male moves his arms independently of the trunk. The American male, we are told, also "may subtly wag his hips with a slight right and left presentation with a movement which involves a twist at the base of the thoracic cage and at the ankles."

Birdwhistell is also responsible (together with the Interdisciplinary Committee on Culture and Communication of the University of Louisville) for a fascinating attempt at quantitative analysis of what is termed the "courtship dance" of the American adolescent. This singular research project—which in less respectable hands might seem to border on the voyeuristic—delineated exactly 24 steps between the initial tactile contact of the typical pair of young lovers and the terminal act of coition. Moreover, the successive steps and countersteps were seen to have something of a "coercive" or mandatory quality— that is, each step had its necessary forerunner and the sequence could not easily be altered without upsetting the delicate rhythm of the *pas de deux*. For example, the boy, on taking the girl's hand, must wait for the counterpressure of her palm before moving on to the next step of intertwining fingers; and these moves, according to protocol, must occur before the boy may "casually" place his arm around her shoulder. Furthermore, each of these gestures and countergestures should take place before the first kiss. Incidentally, it was found that the familiar terms "fast" and "slow" have to do not with the amount of time taken at each stage but with the proper ordering of the sequences; thus, to skip steps or reverse their order is seen as "fast," whereas failure to respond to a signal to move on is "slow." But the actual time involved in the ritual is extremely variable; according to Birdwhistell, "the courtship dance, in clock time, is probably as short as an hour or as long as several years."

The evidence of this description, and of others like it, strongly suggests that there is an unwritten "etiquette" governing important aspects of interpersonal and social relations—a tacit code of conduct and communication learned informally and for the most part unconsciously, much as the child acquires the basic grammar and structure of his native language apart from formal instruction. Indeed it may be, as some anthropologists have conjectured, that within every organized society there are "two cultures": one an authorized version, so to speak, expressed in the mores and morals; the other unauthorized and unconscious, expressed in the folkways. The two may be in harmony or in disharmony; the etiquette described by the courtship dance is hardly the etiquette prescribed by Emily Post. But both of these, ritual and rule alike, are equally products of culture—learned behaviors that are functionally adaptive to the strains and stringencies of social life. Because both are acquired, not innate, characteristics, it would be reckless to regard either of the codes as more "natural" or "authentic" than the other; for what may appear natural (good, true, or beautiful) to one society may be decidedly unnatural (evil, false, or repugnant) to another. The wisdom of the "folk" (or of the "blood" or of the "race") may be older than the knowledge of the *polis*; it might even on occasion prove to be wiser, as in the drama of Antigone and Creon. But modern evidence of its invocation and veneration, such as the Teutonic regression of Nazi Germany, demonstrates that it can also be intolerant, ignorant, and ignoble. The efforts of science to decipher the subliminal codes of interpersonal conduct, notably those of kinesics and proxemics, have made a positive contribution to our understanding of the human connection; but they do not, so far as we are now aware, present or portend a breakthrough to a higher consciousness or a deeper truth.

With respect to the kinesic analysis of courtship behavior and gender display, there is another specific *caveat* which prominent researchers such as Birdwhistell and Scheflen have been careful to emphasize. It is, simply, that gender-related signals between the sexes do not invariably convey a sexual intent; as in other fields of human functioning, appearances are often deceptive and nonverbal messages cannot always be taken at face value. It is true, as Birdwhistell observes, "that in certain contexts gender display, appropriately responded to, is an

essential element in the complex interchange between humans preliminary to courtship, to coitus,
and, even, to mating." However, it is equally true
that in other contexts gender display has very different meanings: It may be nonsexual (as in a business
meeting), pseudosexual (a public dance or performance), or even antisexual—e.g., "the male can pre-
vent coitus and even courtship from occurring by
presenting in a manner which defines his action as
insufficiently directed to the receiving female."

Scheflen has given the label of "quasi-courtship
behavior" to the various manifestations of gender
display which are not evidently aimed at mating,
coupling, or courting. On the basis of content analyses of numerous sound films taken at psychotherapy
sessions, business meetings, and other male-female
encounters, Scheflen concluded that a consistent pattern of postural and gestural activity resembling
courtship behavior was on display in all of these
settings. His system of classification falls into four
categories. "Courtship readiness" involves a preparatory set of more or less involuntary functions
such as changes in muscle and skin tone, alert and
attentive posture, disappearance of body sag and
slouching, and a general tightening up. "Preening
behavior" indicates more volitional acts such as
stroking or combing the hair, adjusting clothes, ties
and socks, glancing in the mirror, and so on. "Positional cues" refer to the directional arrangement of
bodies and limbs by which a couple become mutually oriented and tend to block others out of the
tête-à-tête; thus they may lean forward, use their
arms to close a circle, and cross legs or feet toward

each other. "Actions of appeal or invitation" are illustrated, in the case of females, by such nonverbal cues as flirtatious glances, direct and sustained eye contact, rolling the hips, crossing the legs to expose part of a thigh, displaying a wrist or palm, protruding the breasts, and others.

While these are the characteristics of genuine courtship behavior, Scheflen found them to be prevalent also in nonsexual encounters between males and females—the difference being expressed in slight and subtle distinctions in the manner of signaling. Often these qualifications are conveyed through the transmission of mixed messages; thus, while the positional cues of head and leg angles may signal an exclusive twosome, the trunk of the body may be turned away from the partner and arms opened out to include others within the group. Another method of denying courtship intention is to omit a key step or phase of the gender signals, leaving the message incomplete or ambiguous. Indeed, an element of ambiguity may well be an intrinsic part of the games people play, unconsciously as well as consciously. It might be ventured as a mere speculation that in many male-female encounters, however sober-sided and businesslike the manifest content, there is a latent dimension of sexual interest and stimulus: a flash of fantasy, a moment of promise, a hint of irrelevant possibilities. So, at least, our imaginative literature has often informed us—although, to be sure, it has also warned us of the consequences of misinterpretation.

And would it have been worth it, after all,
After the cups, the marmalade, the tea,

Among the porcelain, among some talk of you and me,
Would it have been worth while,
To have bitten off the matter with a smile,
To have squeezed the universe into a ball
To roll it toward some overwhelming question, . . .
If one, settling a pillow by her head,
> Should say: "That is not what I meant at all;
> That is not it at all."[11]

EXPRESSIONS: FACE VALUE

The great silent film actor Lon Chaney, Sr., who was especially adept at assuming masks of horror, made his reputation as "the man of a thousand faces." But, in a real sense, so are we all. It is not just that we are forever making faces, putting on a face, pulling a face, and preparing a face to meet the faces that we meet. It is rather that the skin of the face—like the face of the skin (see Chapter 4)—is the most flexible, versatile, and shifty piece of equipment in our anatomical inventory. Birdwhistell has estimated that the human face is capable of assuming some 250,000 different expressions; while that may be excessive (who could tabulate such a number?), the most conservative estimate of physiologists defines us all as men and women of many thousand faces.

However, if the human face can speak volumes, it is not always an open book. Unlike much of nonverbal communication, facial expressions are largely under conscious control. "Since we are aware of the communicative potential of our face," as Mark L. Knapp points out, "we tend to monitor it carefully—inhibiting when desired and exhibiting when desired." We are taught early in life to mask certain emotions; and we learn almost as soon to feign others. "For I can smile, and murder whilst I smile," declared the infamous Duke who was to become Richard III; "and wet my cheek with artificial tear, . . . and frame my face to all occasions."

Even though we exercise considerable control over the display of facial expressions, the controls are not always conscious; having been acquired in early life, they become habitual and may often be exhibited without intention—or even against intention.

The face performs a number of expressive and communicative functions in human life, not all of them mutually consistent. Second only to speech as a channel of communication, the face provides a kind of visual reinforcement or punctuation accompanying the spoken word, as well as a source of feedback or acknowledgment of the speech of others. Facial expressions also, of course, reveal emotional states and register attitudes toward others; thus when we are seeking someone's approval we tend to smile and nod our head more than when we are avoiding approval (a less frequent behavior, to be sure).

That facial expressions may be not only overlapping but also contradictory was discovered by researchers in the process of running films of therapeutic encounters at slow motion, when it became apparent that there was more going on facially than met the naked eye. The films revealed very subtle expressions which appear and disappear so rapidly as to pass undetected in normal interaction. Specifically, when films were run at four frames (rather than the normal 24) per second, two and a half times as many changes of expression could be observed. At normal projection speed only those expressions which took longer than two fifths of a second were usually identifiable; those which endured about two fifths of a second could be noticed but not specified; and those which lasted only one fifth of a second were not seen at all. It was speculated that these micromomentary flashes of expression represent emotions which slip out unbidden from behind the mask, as it were, and are quickly suppressed or censored; accordingly they are often inconsistent with what a person is "trying to say." Knapp has cited an instance from this research: "One patient, saying nice things about a friend, had a seemingly pleasant facial expression; slow motion films revealed a wave of anger cross her face."

Some 32 distinctive kinemes or movements of the face and head have been identified by Birdwhistell and his collaborators, involving such features as the whole head, brow, eyelids, nose, mouth, and chin. Three variations on the head nod were observed (the "one nod," "two nod," and "three nod"), along with two lateral head sweeps ("one sweep" and "two sweep"), three movements of the entire head, and a set of three which entail raising the head, lowering it, and holding it steady. The brow yielded four separate kinemes: designated as lifted, lowered, knit, and single-brow movement.

Research on eyelid behavior produced the finding that there are four significant degrees of lid closure: "overopen," "slit," "closed," and "squeezed." The phenomenon known as "laugh lines" (contraction of the skin around the eyes) proved somewhat recalcitrant to analysis; as Birdwhistell prudently put it, "We have not yet been able to determine whether this distal crinkling has kinemic status. It is clear that its absence significantly varies the 'meaning' of a smile or laugh, but until we can demonstrate that it is not merely an allokine of lid closure, we must withhold its assignment."

Moving on down the face, the researchers found the nose to be the locus of four distinct behaviors ("wrinkle-nose," "compressed nostrils," "bilateral nostril flare," and "unilateral nostril flare or closure"); while the mouth, marvelously expressive but subtle in its maneuvers, yielded a set of seven tentative descriptions—namely, "compressed lips," "protruded lips," "retracted lips," "apically withdrawn lips," "snarl," "lax open mouth," and "mouth over-open." Other facial kinemes included puffed cheeks and sucked cheeks and two different thrusts of the chin (anterior and lateral), with the added possibility of the "chin drop" gaining status as a distinct kineme.

The relationship of these small physiognomic exhibitions, and of the several parts of the face, to the expression of particular emotions has been fruitfully investigated by P. Ekman, who devised a coding system (the Facial Affect Scoring Technique, or FAST) to deal with six basic emotions: happiness, anger, surprise, sadness, disgust, and fear. Among his findings were that sadness appears to involve the most facial movements and positions—as many as eight of the brow and forehead, eight of the eyes and lids, and ten of the lower face. By and large the lower face was thought to produce a greater number of expressive positions than the upper brow area. More significantly, perhaps, the FAST coding indicates that emotions are not registered evenly across the facial map but are concentrated in specific areas; for example, the lower face and the area of the eyes are the most prominent indicators of happiness, the eyes have it with regard to sadness, the lower face together with the brow-forehead especially reflects anger, while disgust is concentrated in the lower face, and the eye area and lower face are reliable predictors of surprise.

Other studies have produced roughly similar correlations between emotional states and particular facial cues. Harrison asked his subjects to interpret drawings of faces with deliberately varied positioning of eyebrows, eyelids, and mouth. The subjects associated raised brows with surprise, half-raised brows with worry, and a single raised brow with disbelief; the eyes when wide open suggested alertness and when half closed were seen as boredom, while a turned-up mouth conveyed happiness and a turned-down mouth signaled distress. In another study the combination of lowered brows and up-turned mouth was interpreted as "fiendish." Argyle has reported that other facial movements have similar associations; thus, rapid blinking is taken to reveal anxiety.

Two important qualifications should, however, be noted concerning these refined analyses of microphysiological behavior. The first is that single positions or movements cannot be sensibly interpreted apart from the larger context of behavior and culture in which they occur; wrinkling of the nose, for example, may signify a variety of emotions ranging from revulsion to affection. The second reservation is that the expression of emotions is both a subjective experience and an intersubjective communication; there is not only an actor who is "emoting" but, for the most part, an audience which is interpreting. Facial expressions represent cues to anyone who may be watching; and the perception of such cues is always selective, varying with personality and past associations as well as with culture.

A graphic illustration of cultural relativity (and cultural clash) in the meanings ascribed to gestures of the head has been provided by the noted linguist Roman Jakobson, in a discussion of nonverbal signs for "yes" and "no." The episode relates the utter confusion experienced by a group of Russians and Bulgarians, thrown together in a nineteenth-century confrontation, as a result of what appeared to be diametrically opposed head motions for affirmation and negation in use by the two nations. The Russians employed the same sign system as the Americans and most European peoples—i.c., a nod of the head for "yes" and a sideward shake of the head for "no." The Bulgarians practiced what looked like the exact opposite (although, on close analysis, subtle differences were detectable): shaking the head for "yes" and nodding the head for "no." Predictably, conversations between the two groups were continually thrown off the track, and a sort of Balkan comedy of errors ensued—which was not quite resolved even when the source of the difficulty became clear. For even when the Russians switched to Bulgarian style, the Bulgarians could never be certain that a given Russian had done so.

GOOD LOOKS AND EVIL EYES

As the face may be regarded as the central registry of mood and emotion, so the eyes are at the center of the facial countenance. Although much of significance goes on in the brows and lids above them, and still more in the mouth and chin below, it is the eyes that "focus" this activity and on which the attention of others is in turn focused. The behaviors of the moving eye, its strategies and diplomacies, are remarkable in their variety and complexity. Although kinesicists have found it comparatively simple to catalogue gross movements of the eye, and while certain functions (such as dilation and contraction of the pupil) appear to be innate and hence universally recognizable, the eyes are peculiarly expressive of individual personality. Human eyes may stare, glare, glance, gaze, scan, appraise, survey, contemplate, or scrutinize; they may roll, dart, flash, light up, darken, redden, turn inward, wink, wince, loll, and liquefy; they may appear to hypnotize, fascinate, lure, seduce, dare, defy, defile, throw daggers, wither, and even kill. But none of these familiar and fabled acts is ever performed in quite the same way by any two sets of eyes. We not only look different from one another; we look differently.

The symbolism that has accumulated around the human eye is rich and colorful. It is also largely ominous—a curious fact in view of the attractive aspects of the eye and its evident role in sociability. The metaphor of "the look that kills" has its origin in widespread superstitions concerning the "evil eye" (*mal de ojo* in Spanish), such as the belief of Middle American Indians that certain persons can produce dire effects by staring at children and the reported conviction of South African bushmen that one look from the eye of a menstruating girl can stop a man in his tracks and turn him into a tree.

In other cultures it is not the look that kills but the act of looking that gets one killed—as in the salty tale of Lot's wife. Where one does not perish at the sight of whatever it is that is forbidden, one can expect to be put to death for certain visual violations; for example, in some Asian countries it was a capital offense to lay eyes on the royal personage or embodied divinity. These ancient strictures governing the act of looking, though greatly modified, still survive in attenuated form in the unconscious rituals of interpersonal encounter—not merely in the common act of "shutting our eyes" to certain spectacles but in the delicate uses and non-uses of eye contact in everyday life: holding or withholding glances, looking up or down (or up-and-down), scanning the scene, sizing up the situation, or not taking the slightest notice.

As Ashcroft and Scheflen point out in their valuable study of *People Space*, looking is a form of behavior we all perform thousands of times every day but rarely pay attention to: "Yet this little behavior itself contributes to orderly relations by defining boundaries of interaction." As we have seen in previous chapters, there are rules of decorum and rites of passage accompanying everyday encounters which require a tacit understanding of when it is proper to engage others visually and when to disengage. Strangers passing on a street will recognize each other's presence by a quick glance, at the appropriate distance (about 10 to 12 feet); they will then immediately look away, in the polite ritual that Goffman has termed civil inattention. What they are doing is to acknowledge each other's private space and to signal their policy of noninterference. "In Western culture, holding eye contact invites engagement. Looking away discourages it." Those strangers who try to "catch one's eye" and hold it, thus violating the gentleman's agreement, are seen as intruders with an untoward purpose in mind—commonly a form of solicitation.

When people move into a territory not their own, as when they are guests entering a home or visitors to an office, "they will act out a series of behaviors that customarily include the dropping of the head and eyes." This deferential gesture apparently serves as a kind of minuscule bow, as if to soften the presence of the interloper; on the other hand the owner of the territory is likely not to drop his own eyes but to stare straight ahead and even to glare if he should perceive the entrance as an intrusion. Again, when a stranger passes by a group of people he will tend to look down or away as he steps quickly by. If he finds it necessary to move through the center of the group, instead of around it, he will look fixedly ahead while murmuring a verbal excuse. It is evident that the significance of a look varies with direction and duration, among other things; a momentary glance is less personal and challenging than a prolonged stare, while looking down or away from another is more deferential than looking directly at him. To be sure, these conventions are sometimes defied or turned around; thus, while averting eyes has traditionally signaled subordinate status or inferior social class, the refusal to do so may be part of a conscious strategy of resistance or rebellion. Goffman offers an example of this behavior in the case of lower-class Mexican-American youth gangs, among whom "the notion of a 'bad look' seems fairly well-established, involving an infraction of the rule that subordinates are supposed to avert their gaze after having returned the superordinate's for a brief time."

The manifold niceties and nuances of public eye behavior—which include such problems as when not to look, where not to look, and how to appear not to be looking—have intrigued various students of the human scene. Goffman has observed that "penetration of the eyes" is such a common, if subtle, form of territorial intrusion that there is a constant and great need of "eye discipline." Among the more delicate situations in which this visual self-control is called for are those interpersonal contacts related to gender display and appreciation. Ashcroft and Scheflen tell us what we may already know but do not often reflect on:

There are spots or areas on and around the human body which may be looked at and others which are taboo. Some spots may be looked at in one instance and not in another. A woman sitting on a couch during a conversation may display her knee and calf. Within certain limits of etiquette, the other participants may be permitted to glance at, but probably not stare at, the display. She

makes this specific portion of her body public. In so doing, she does not suspend the rules of privacy to include
other parts of her body, nor does she invite others to
touch this body spot or make comments about it. Should
she notice a male staring at her breasts, she may recognize this violation by glancing at him and glancing away.
. . . The violator would probably be respecting her
claim should he rub his eyes and turn them away from
the spot, as males are accustomed to do when caught
looking where they shouldn't be looking.[12]

Goffman has added on this general subject that, in
middle-class society, nakedness particularly calls out
the trained capacity for discipline and discretion in
the use of the eyes—as in the effort displayed by
nudist-camp residents to appear not to notice each
other's erogenous zones. "A rule in our society:
when bodies are naked, glances are clothed."

The eyes are there not only for seeing; they are
also there to be seen. From time immemorial they
have been objects of fascination, often of awe, occasionally of reverence. They have also been feared—
not only in myths of the evil eye but in tales (sometimes true) of their hypnotic power, in fantasies and
dreams which transform them into sexual organs,
and in fables relating their ability to penetrate masks
and surfaces (e.g., Superman's X-ray vision) and
thereby to read innermost thoughts or lay bare the
soul. Persons with something to hide, or with feelings of guilt or shame, tend to avoid the eyes of
others and to convert their innocent looks into acts of
peeping, peeking, peering, and spying. Historically
those who were suspected of such voyeuristic activity have frequently had their eyes put out. The

ritual of blinding in fact is a common motif in the folklore of various cultures; in the Greek myths, for example, Orion was blinded for the act of rape and Stesichorus for reviling Helen of Troy, while Oedipus took his own sight as self-punishment for acting out his Freudian complex.

But the images of the eye, in folk and literate culture, are by no means wholly negative; there are good looks as well as evil eyes. Poets have labored to capture in words our intuitive apprehension of the reflections in a golden eye—most of all the eye of a woman and even more especially the eye of the beloved. The most common images are those of light—illuminating, sparkling, darting rays, and occasionally flaming. The Book of Matthew proclaimed that "the light of the body is the eye"; Thomas Moore made a lyric of "The light that lies/ In woman's eyes"; Du Bartas addressed "These lovely lamps, these windows of the soul"; and Shakespeare, characteristically, in *Love's Labor's Lost*, elevated the sphere of light into that of enlightenment:

> For where is any author in the world
> Teaches such beauty as a woman's eye? . . .

> From women's eyes this doctrine I derive:
> They sparkle still the right Promethean fire;
> They are the books, the arts, the academes,
> That show, contain, and nourish all the world.

Nowadays it is not only poets and lovers who are intrigued with the conduct and caprices of the human eye; physiologists, psychologists, and a variety of social scientists are equally devoted to the subject, although to be sure from the standpoint of detached observers rather than bemused participants. A number of recent developments have converged to produce a new trend toward more systematic and controlled observation of gazes and glances—among them the influence of ethology with its attention to the expressions and orienting movements of animals, the rapid growth of the "silent language" disciplines such as kinesics and proxemics, and the increasing use of film and videotape records in both therapeutic and experimental settings, which permit close-up measurement of even "micromomentary" flickers and flashes. As Argyle and Kendon have summarized:

We may distinguish three ways in which visual orientation functions in interactions: 1) to look at another is a social act in itself; 2) to meet the gaze of another is a significant event and may often be an important part of the goal sought in interaction; 3) in seeing another, much important information about him may be gathered, in addition to his direction of gaze.[13]

In another study Kendon divided the functions of gazing into four groups: *cognitive* (as when one looks away in the process of working out a thought); *monitoring* (as a check on the attentiveness or interest of another); *regulatory* (as a control on interaction), and *expressive* (signaling mood or attitude). Several of these functions may be involved in a given instance of gaze behavior; for example, a speaker wishing feedback in conversation generally raises his eyes to the listener's to signal the end of an utterance, to elicit a response, to see if the other is listening, and possibly to dominate or reassure the addressee. The listener in his turn may meet the glance either reassuringly or defiantly; if he looks away, it may mean that he is bored or that he is intently pondering the utterance—or alternatively that he is angry, apprehensive, embarrassed, or distracted by a more compelling sight.

Our eyes not only "take the measure" of another; they also appear to give us a measure of the distance or intimacy we desire. Argyle and Janet Dean found that persons wishing to develop a relationship with another sought eye contact and stepped up their looks, but only to a point; too much eye contact on either side created anxiety. This suggested to the researchers that both attraction and avoidance forces are involved in visual interactions, leading to the inference that there is an optimum "equilibrium level" for each encounter, in which the two forces are brought into balance. In short, if two persons wish to be closer, mutual glances increase; if they are too close for comfort, eye contact decreases. People generally appear to be drawn by the gaze of others; experiments by Mario von Cranach and others indicate that both adults and children prefer to approach persons who look at them closely rather than those who look away. It would seem that the eye, almost rivaling the voice, is a primary message center for signals of recognition, assurance, and approval; we look *at* others to appraise them, and we look *to* others for praise of ourselves.

It might safely be concluded, then, that there is more to looking than meets the eye.

GESTURES: SIGN LANGUAGE

The language of gesture—principally involving the arms, hands, and fingers—is older than speech and often nearly as subtle and elaborate. In cultures such as the Japanese, where silence is a virtue, gestures are highly stylized and also graded according to sex, rank, age, and class. Among various North American Indian tribes, which also placed a premium on silence, gestures were refined into explicit sign languages with high symbolic content. As Maurice H. Krout tells us:

The Cheyennes, for example, elaborated a sign system consisting of over 7000 individual items. Indian sign language involved primarily the use of arms and hands. Some of the signs had direct, and some had indirect, symbolic reference. For example, pointing to the mouth could refer to the mouth or it might mean "baby"; pointing skyward either referred to the sky or meant "The Great Mystery" or, simply, "today." In spite of these complications, the Indian sign languages had a great deal in common, and a Plains Indian could successfully communicate with a member of the Iroquois Confederation.[14]

Although gestures are most often employed as graphic accompaniments of speech, serving to illustrate and augment the spoken word, the example of Indian sign language demonstrates that gesture can also substitute for speech and nearly match its versatility. Thus the sign language, or finger talk, in use among the deaf has evolved over a period of at least 800 years into a communicative system of considerable complexity and depth. Almost as elaborate are the secret sign languages developed by various monastic communities bound by vows of silence, such as the Trappists (Order of Cistercians of the Strict Observance). The Trappist monks, forbidden with rare exceptions to use oral or written language in communication with one another, devised a complex silent language of more than 400 signs which has been in use for several hundred years; similarly, the Benedictine monks have developed a secret language consisting of some 460 signs.

The pioneer interpreter of body and gesture language, Ray Birdwhistell, has consistently maintained that there are no "natural" or innate gestures which mean the same thing everywhere: ". . . although we have been searching for fifteen years, we have found no gesture of body motion which has the same social meaning in all societies. . . . Insofar as we know, there is no body motion or gesture that can be regarded as a universal symbol." Although this unqualified generalization has been disputed by some researchers—notably ethologists, such as Eibl-Eibesfeldt, whose work with animals has disposed them to instinctual explanations—the weight of the available evidence strongly suggests that cultural variation is more significant than transcultural equivalence in the vocabulary of gestures. The illustrations cited by the anthropologist LaBarre may be taken as representative:

Gestures of contempt are a rich area for study. . . . A favorite Menomini Indian gesture of contempt is to raise the clenched fist palm downward up to the level of the mouth, then bringing it downward quickly and throwing forward the thumb and the first two fingers. Malayan Negritos express contempt or disgust by a sudden expiration of breath, like our "snort of contempt." Neapolitans click the right thumbnail off the right canine in a downward arc. The *mano cornudo* or "making horns" (first and little fingers of the right hand extended forward, thumb and other fingers folded) is primarily used to defy the "evil eye." The *mano fica* (clenched right fist with thumb protruding between the first and second fingers) is an obscene kineme symbolizing the male genitals; in some contexts its meaning is the same as the more massive slapping of the left biceps with the right hand, the left forearm upraised and ending in a fist; a less massive, though no less impolite, equivalent is making a fist with all save the second ("social finger") and thrusting it upward.[15]

LaBarre also takes note of the bewildering variety of ways in which people of different cultures beckon to one another; thus, for example, the Latin American gesture for "come here" is virtually the same as the North American gesture for "get away with you."

In addition to the many gestures which intentionally carry messages, there is a copious category of those which betray their meanings involuntarily. Many of these are on the order of self-comforting gestures, designed to relieve or reduce tension. Sexual differences are especially marked in this area of unintentional behavior. In Western cultures, during states of perplexity or frustration, men will commonly scratch their heads, rub their chins with their hands, tug at the lobes of their ears, or rub their foreheads or cheeks or the back of their necks. Women in similar states tend to behave very differently; they will either put a finger on their lower front teeth with the mouth slightly open or pose a finger under the chin. Other masculine gestures expressing perplexity, not generally shared by women, are: rubbing one's nose, placing the flexed fingers over the mouth, rubbing the side of the neck, rubbing the infraorbital part of the face, rubbing the closed eyes, picking the nose, rubbing the back of the hand or the front of the thigh, and pursing the lips.

Just as students of proxemics have differentiated cultures in terms of high and low "contact," so a kinesicist might grade cultures in terms of the quantity and quality of gestural communication. High on such a list would be the Mediterranean cultures (e.g., the Italians and Greeks), Middle Eastern cultures such as the Arabic, and the Jews of European nations. From the standpoint of northern European cultures, and especially the Anglo-American, the gesticulations of these peoples often appear florid, passionate, and uncomfortably excessive. Even in the pre-Victorian and pre-Puritan age of Shakespeare, English men and women were schooled in the etiquette of restraint. Said Hamlet to the players:

Nor do not saw the air too much with your hand, thus; but use all gently: for in the very torrent, tempest, and as I may say the whirlwind of passion, you must acquire and beget a temperance, that may give it smoothness.

In light of this, it may seem paradoxical that a culture which ranks among the highest in gestural display should also be among the most restrained and least ostentatious in general behavior—namely, the Japanese. There are various explanations for the elaborate gestural repertoire of the Japanese: for example, the unusual degree of respect for silence, influenced by Zen Buddhism, which encourages non-verbal communication; the preference for indirect and oblique means of expression as opposed to forth-right statement; and a fondness for stylized motion, as in the traditional forms of theater and dance. Whatever the reasons, Japanese gestural behavior has become a favorite hunting ground for students of silent communication, as well as for Western visitors seeking to minimize the gaffes and miscues common to encounters with the Japanese. J. Seward, for example, in a chapter devoted to sign language in Japan, lists some twenty-eight ways in which the Japanese commonly employ gestures of the hands and fingers; he also points out that each of the five fingers has a distinctive symbolic label (e.g., the thumb is the parent finger and the littlest is the child finger).

Similar lists and litanies detailing the gestural characteristics of a particular culture or subculture are rapidly accumulating as the literature of kinesics, proxemics, and nonverbal communication generally gains alike in scholarly attention and popular interest. It is well, however, to be reminded once again that the motor habits and muscular exertions which constitute the study of body movement rarely, if ever, have independent meaning but acquire their significance (that which the sign signifies) in the context of social interaction. The primal form of interaction—the prototype of all relationship—is physical contact. Touching is, in a real sense, the completion of the gesture and the object of reaching out. Let us, then, turn our attention to that original human connection.

4 | TOUCHING: The Language of the Skin

We need the comrade heart
That understands,
And the warmth, the living warmth
Of human hands.

—Thomas Curtis Clark

We in the Western world are slowly beginning to discover (more accurately, to rediscover) our neglected senses. This growing awareness represents something of an overdue reaction against the painful deprivation of sensory experience we have long suffered. The impersonality of life in our modern world has become such that we have in effect produced a new race of Untouchables. We have become strangers to one another, not merely avoiding but actively warding off all forms of "unnecessary" physical contact. The ability of Western man to relate to his fellow humans has lagged far behind his ability to converse with computers, commune with cars, and talk with toys. He can reach out to other planets and meticulously monitor the blips of deep space, yearning for a close encounter of an alien kind; but too often he will not reach out to his neighbor, and he does not hear the voice of his own child. His personal frontiers seldom permit the trespass of a deeply felt communication across them. The human dimension is thus contracted and constrained; for through what other avenues than our senses are we able to enter into the dimension of human existence? It is our senses that frame the body of reality.

The world of Western man has increasingly relied for purposes of communication on the "distance senses"—sight and hearing. The "proximity senses"—touch, taste, smell, the vestibular and joint-muscle senses—have either been tabooed, disparaged, or ignored. Seeking palpable proofs and certifiable evidence—governed by norms of bureaucratic efficiency, scientific detachment, and logical abstraction—we have assiduously cultivated the distance senses (verbal, vocal, and visual) to the detriment of the other vital senses which enhance proximity and establish the human connection.

The most humanizing, and in many respects the most crucial, of all of the senses is that of touch. As J. Lionel Tayler observed more than half a century ago:

The greatest sense in our body is our touch sense. It is probably the chief sense in the processes of sleeping and waking; it gives us our knowledge of depth or thickness and form; we feel, we love and hate, are touchy and are touched, through the touch corpuscles of our skin.[1]

THE MIND OF THE SKIN

The skin is the external nervous system of the organism; this is not a metaphor but a fact. The skin, in common with the central nervous system, arises from the outermost of the three embryonic cell layers, the ectoderm. The ectoderm constitutes the general surface covering of the embryonic body. It also gives rise to the hair, teeth, the sense organs of smell, taste, hearing, vision, and touch—everything involved with informing the organism of what goes on outside it. The central nervous system, a principal function of which is the organization of response to the information thus obtained, develops as the inturned portion of the general surface of the embryonic body. The remainder of the surface covering, after the differentiation of the brain, spinal cord, and all the other parts of the central nervous system, is, then, an inturned part of the skin, and the skin remains as the exposed or external portion of the nervous system. Thinking of the skin this way would improve our understanding of it. As Frederic Wood Jones, the brilliant English anatomist, put it, "He is the wise physician and philosopher who realizes that in regarding the external appearance of his fellow-men he is studying the external nervous system and not merely the skin and its appendages."

As the largest and most ancient sense organ of the body, the skin enables the organism to learn about its environment. It is the medium, in all its differentiated parts, by which the external world is perceived. The face and the skin, as sense organs, not only communicate to the brain a knowledge of the external environment but also convey to others within that environment certain information concerning the individual's internal nervous system and mind.

In the average adult, the skin occupies about 18,000 square centimeters, or approximately 18 square feet, and weighs about eight pounds, constituting 16 to 18 percent of total body weight. A piece of skin the size of a quarter contains more than three million cells, 12 feet of nerves, 100 sweat glands, 50 nerve endings, and three feet of blood vessels. It is estimated that there are about 50 receptors per 100 square centimeters, a total of 900,000 sensory receptors. Tactile points vary from seven to 135 per square centimeter. The number of sensory fibers entering the spinal cord is well over half a million.

In other words, the skin is a giant communications system which, through the sense of touch, brings the signals and messages of the external environment to the attention of that internal environment which, for want of a better word, we call the mind. In short, in whatever manner a person or a physical event affects an individual by touch is evaluated both in the nervous and mental systems of the individual. The latter will then react in a relatively simple way to the stimulus—that is, with behavior involving either little or no conscious thought, or else with a *response* to the stimulus. The term "response" is here used in contrast to "reaction" to imply that the signal has been consciously decoded before any behavioral response is made to it.

It is the skin that is the earliest of the sensory organs to come into being, and it is through the skin that the baby receives its first communications. In the womb the conceptus has been the recipient of tactile communications from its earliest days. These communications are maximized during the experience of birth—an experience which lasts for some 14 hours on the average in the first-born and some eight hours on the average in the subsequent-born. There is evidence that the massive stimulation of the skin received during labor plays an important role in preparing the baby for postnatal existence. It has long been known to animal breeders, and those experienced with farm animals, that unless the mother vigorously licks her newly born young, they are likely to die from failure of the gastrointestinal and genitourinary tracts to function.

Human mothers do not, however, lick their young; the prolonged period of labor renders that unnecessary, for the cutaneous stimulation produced by the contractions of the uterus on the body of the fetus performs the work that licking does in other mammals.

We can check this theory by observing what happens when, in humans, the baby is born in the absence of labor, either precipitately or by cesarean section. What, in such cases, would we expect to find? Most obviously we would expect to find a significant difference in gastrointestinal and genitourinary conditions. Were we knowledgeable enough we would also expect to find differences in respiratory-tract functions, for stimulation of the skin—as most of us are aware under the impact of a sudden shower of cold water—as an activator of the respiratory system is considerable.

Dr. Mary Shirley found that prematurely born infants achieve bowel and bladder control with greater difficulty and later than do full-term children. Dr. Cecil Drillien and other researchers have found that infections of the upper respiratory tract are significantly more frequent in prematures than in term-born children. It has long been known that, when a baby is not breathing after it has been born, a few slaps on the buttocks or general body massage will usually succeed in initiating respiration. The same result can be accomplished by placing the baby alternately in hot and cold baths. The stimulation of the skin by such methods is generally sufficient to start respiration. Mere stroking of the body will have the same effect.

For the whole of human evolutionary history, if we are to judge from the practice in existing food-gathering–hunting societies, almost immediately after birth the baby was placed to nurse at the mother's breast. With their naked bodies in contact, the nursing couple enlarged and deepened the scope of their reciprocal communications, the baby receiving as many benefits as he bestowed on his mother. On his part the baby receives invaluable tactile benefits, such as the stabilization of his body temperature (which had suffered a precipitous fall at his birth), gamma globulins that immunize him against viral and bacterial infections, gastrointestinal and genitourinary activating stimuli, which provide him with the ideal food adjusted to the development of his metabolic abilities, and—most importantly— engage him in a dialogue with his mother which is the beginning of a socialization process that cannot be as effectively achieved in any other way. As Gough has pointed out, the early basis of communi-cation in the human species appears to be involved with feeding. The compulsive fixation of the baby's eyes on the mother's face strongly suggests that the feeding situation may be an interpersonal dialogue with implications for optimum development of communication. Such a dialogue has, indeed, been shown to occur between mother and infant.

Physically, the baby at his mother's breast bestows benefits on her which are quite as remarkable as those she confers upon him. When a baby begins to nurse at the mother's breast he initiates sensory changes in her neurohumoral system. The pituitary gland responds by secreting two important hormones, prolactin and oxytocin. Prolactin produces a general maternalizing effect on the mother, it stimulates the flow of milk into the breast and sustains lactation, and it inhibits ovulation. Oxytocin assists in the release of milk from the alveoli of the breast into the ducts, called "the letdown reflex," and it also produces massive contractions of the uterus and constriction of the uterine blood vessels, thus arresting the post-partum hemorrhage, initiating the return of the uterus to normal size (which, in the absence of a suckling baby, it will never achieve), and, finally, the completion of the third stage of labor—the detachment and ejection of the placenta. These facts are mentioned because they happen to be the three most serious problems with which the obstetrician may be confronted after the birth of a baby. Where the obstetrician's own methods fail in dealing with these difficulties, the baby put to nurse at his mother's breast will usually solve them within five to ten minutes.

The benefits mutually bestowed on each other by the nursing pair are innumerable. We have mentioned only a few which indicate the fundamental importance of tactile communication for the physical well-being of both infant and mother. The psychological benefits the nursing couple confer on each other are immense. For example, it has now been demonstrated that for healthy bonding to be established between mother and child this should be as soon after the baby's birth as possible. For this to transpire the mother and baby should, of course, be together virtually from the moment of birth. Such bonding should also involve the father and siblings. It is a great mark of progress that hospitals in many parts of the United States, recognizing that pregnancy and the birth of a baby are family affairs, are now converting their obstetrical divisions into Family Care Centers and in a number of cases are so labeling them. In such centers the environment is made as homelike as possible, and the members of the family are not only invited but encouraged to stay there until the mother and baby are ready to leave.

Paralleling this movement, and antedating it, is the Home Birth Movement. Here the emphasis is on birth as a communion which is best celebrated in the bosom of the family and not in a dehumanized, over-technologized environment presided over by over-trained and overspecialized technicians. With pre-natal care, overseen by obstetricians, the Home Birth Movement rightly prefers midwives to help mothers bring their children safely and happily into the world.

In the civilized lands of the world, those with the most advanced obstetrics, the maternal and infant morbidity and mortality rates are lower for home births than for hospital deliveries. And this, we may suspect, is not entirely due to the possibility that the home is a cleaner place than the hospital. It is probable that the socio-psychological environment in the home—the familiar surroundings and faces, the nonseparation of mother and child, their intimate association with each other and what passes between them during that association—contribute substantially to the difference in morbidity and mortality rates in favor of home births.

The need of the young human for cutaneous stimulation is but a continuation of the need he has so abundantly enjoyed in the womb. Reinforced by the massive stimulation he received during labor, his need for communication in the complex world into which he has abruptly been introduced has grown even greater. While his other senses are quite functional, the principal means at his disposal for receiving signals and messages from the world around him is through tactile stimulation. The baby who is held closely, cuddled, caressed, and treated as nearly as possible as he was treated when he was still in the womb is reassured. After what he may well have experienced as the trauma of birth, he comes once more into safe harbor in the reassuring arms of a loving mother. This kind of communication, the message of reassurance, is of the utmost significance to the baby.

Bodily warmth and contact are not, of course, the only sensual pleasures of importance to the child. Small babies, for example, love to be bathed, and as children grow older many mothers use the bath almost as a specific remedy for childhood ills. Such baths and the caressing accompanying them soothe not only the body but the spirit. The reassurance gained from body contact with the mother can be a determining factor in the baby's development into childhood.

Testimony from another culture—one that we still miscall "primitive"—shows us the kind of relationship between mother and child that we in the West have long since left behind us, perhaps not altogether to our advantage. Kabongo, an 80-year-old African chief of the Kikuyu tribe, recalling his childhood, speaks:

My early years are connected in my mind with my mother. At first she was always there; I can remember the comforting feel of her body as she carried me on her back, and the smell of her skin in the hot sun. Everything came from her. When I was hungry or thirsty she would swing me round to where I could reach her full breasts; now when I shut my eyes I feel again with gratitude the sense of well-being that I had when I buried my head in their softness and drank the sweet milk that they gave me. At night when there was no sun to warm me, her arms, her body, took its place; and as I grew older and more interested in other things, from my safe place on her back I could watch without fear as I wanted, and when sleep overcame me, I had only to close my eyes.[2]

As the baby grows he begins to touch everything. This is a primary way of learning. He sees an object, but he is not satisfied until he feels it, too. He must know what this object is like through the communications he receives from his skin before he will accept it. It is almost as if an object was not real until it had been verified by touch. The act of touching also

teaches the baby his first lessons in learning his identity. In the beginning he does not differentiate
sharply, if at all, between himself and his environment, but very soon he begins to make distinctions.
These lessons will continue throughout his life, becoming more complex as he grows older, reaching
out to something that is not himself and touching it.
This development was clearly understood by Ten-
nyson, who wrote, in his great lyric poem "In
Memoriam":

> The baby new to earth and sky
> What time his tender palm is prest
> Against the circle of the breast,
> Has never thought that "this is I."
>
> But as he grows he gathers much,
> And learns the use of "I" and "me,"
> And finds "I am not what I see,
> And other than the things I touch."
>
> So rounds he to a separate mind
> From whence clear memory may begin,
> As thro' the frame that binds him in
> His isolation grows defined.
>
> This use may lie in blood and breath,
> Which else were fruitless of their due,
> Had man to learn himself anew
> Beyond the second birth of Death.

Particularly important in the development of the
child is the growth of his affection for other people
and his ability to express that affection. And here the
sense of touch is perhaps most crucial to his future
happiness. For in addition to receiving messages, he
soon begins to send messages. When his feelings are
aroused they are at first communicated through

touching. He pats his mother's breast. As Spurgeon English has said, "Love and touch are indivisible." Touch, said Alexander Bain, the English psychologist, is the alpha and omega of affection.

A TOUCH OF CULTURE

Just as there are wide differences between individuals in their ability to express affection and love through physical contact, so there are variations between societies. The peoples of the Anglo-Saxon linguistic group—English, German, and American—are very much less "demonstrative" in the expression of affection than are the peoples of the Romance-language group—Italians, French, and Spanish. Among Anglo-Saxons there are also striking class differences in the tactile expression of affection, the rule being: the higher the class, the lower the ability to express oneself through touch. In Victorian times, upper-class boys were taught that demonstrations of affection were "unmanly." A virtuous woman never allowed a man to touch her, unless she was married to him or at least engaged; she was expected to shrink from unsolicited contact. An accidental touch was a trespass upon one's person and privacy, and the offender was expected to apologize for it, even to members of his own family. Moreover, the bare skin was decidedly sinful—so much so that women were often prevailed upon to wear a slip when bathing in order to protect them against the sight of their own naked bodies.

The conditioning received by many Anglo-Saxons who were brought up in such nontactility produced a virtual negative sanction against touch. This was so much the case that the sense of touch and the act of touching came to be culturally defined as vulgar. The public demonstration of affection was vulgar, touching was vulgar, and only men who were quite outside the pale—such as Latins, Russians, and the like—would ever dream of putting their arms around each other, not to mention indulging in such effeminacies as kissing each other on the cheek.

It is of more than passing interest to note that in England the National Guidance Council on Marriage, in one of its publications some years ago, suggested that the rising divorce rate was due largely to a lack of physical contact in the English family. Small boys, it reported, were admonished not to embrace their mothers during some little crisis but to remain manly by maintaining "a stiff upper lip." The Council advised that the English "need to touch, stroke, and comfort one another more often."

Even more advanced in nontactility than the English and Americans are the Germans. The traditional emphasis on the warrior virtues, the hard-headed martinet father, and the subordination of the mother and other females in the German family made for a rigidified, unbending character that has rendered the average German, among other things, a not very tactile creature.

Interestingly, Austrian males tend to be tactually more demonstrative and will embrace close friends, whereas in Germany this is a relatively rare occurrence except among males of Jewish extraction.

The Jews, as a tribe, culture, or people, are characterized by a high degree of tactility. The legendary "Jewish mother" has become a symbol of all-consuming overpossessiveness. What this meant was that until recent times Jewish children were breast-fed on demand and that there was a great deal of fondling by mother, father, and siblings; hence, adult Jews tend to be tactually very demonstrative. For example, it is considered perfectly normal for an adult male to continue to greet his father with a kiss and an embrace and to do so also on parting.

Richard Heslin and Diane Boss have investigated what happens tactually between people being met and seen off at the main airport in Indianapolis. Siblings were found to be quite reserved in their use of touch; males tended to initiate touching more than females in cross-sex pairs; older people initiated touching more than younger people in cross-sex encounters. However, older people did not initiate touching more than younger people in same-sex pairs. Pairs of women gave and received more solid hugs, scored higher on the touch intimacy scale, and touched each other on the head, arm, or back more than did pairs of men; in contrast, pairs of men shook hands more than pairs of women. Departures showed more extended embraces, more intimate touching, and (predictably) sadder facial expressions than did arrivals. Heslin and Boss speculate that at least three factors could be at work here: (a) a desire to retain contact as long as possible, (b) a desire to accumulate some closeness in anticipation of the forthcoming separation, and (c) a sense of freedom from having to maintain that high level of intimacy after the traveler leaves. In different individuals different conditions may of course have been operative. In any event, the second suggestion of the investigators—the accumulation of closeness in anticipation of separation—is of particular interest, for it refers to a behavior that is rarely if ever discussed—that is, the embrace under emotional circumstances as a means of incorporating the other within oneself. In their study, involving 120 women, 86 men, and 103 encounters, Heslin and Boss found that intimate encounters were infrequent, even though the encounters were between relatives in 74 cases, lovers in 12 instances, and friends in 18.

Americans of Anglo-Saxon origin are not quite as untactual as the English or Germans, but they do not lag far behind. American boys neither kiss nor embrace their friends as, for example, do Latin Americans. There are occasions, however, when American males will spontaneously shed their inhibitions, joyfully embrace, and even kiss one another with complete abandon. This is most likely to happen when the players in an athletic contest win an important game or match. The uninhibited hugging on such occasions is something to behold—all the more pleasant to witness because of its utter spontaneity.

Examples of the curious ways in which nontactuality expresses itself may be seen in the behavior of members of the noncontact cultures in various social situations. It has been observed that the way an Anglo-Saxon shakes hands constitutes a signal to the other to keep his proper distance. A similar practice is observable in crowds. For example, in a packed bus or subway, the Anglo-Saxon tends to remain stiff and rigid, with a blank facial expression which seems to deny the existence of the other passengers. As Germaine Greer has remarked, "Crushed against his brother in the Tube the average Englishman pretends desperately that he is alone." The contrast of the scene on the French Métro is striking; here passengers will lean and press against one another, if not without reserve, at least without embarrassment or apology. Often the leaning and lurching will give rise to good-natured laughter and joking, with no attempt made to avoid meeting the eyes of other passengers. A protesting Englishman or American on such occasions is regarded as a more than ordinarily pathetic figure of fun.

Investigators have consistently found that tactile closeness facilitates psychological and interpersonal closeness. D. Aigulera found that nurses were able to communicate more easily with patients whom they touched than with those whom they did not touch. J. E. Pattison discovered that undergraduate females engaged in more verbal self-disclosure when touched at an initial counseling interview than when they were not touched. B. M. Raiche, in a study of children in the first, second, and third grades, found that they responded to the counselor who was seen to touch (in video-taped segments simulating counseling with children) significantly more frequently than to those who refrained from touching.

SEX AND TOUCH

Interesting sex differences were found by T. Nguyen, R. Heslin, and M. L. Nguyen in a study of 41 male and 40 female undergraduates. The males considered pleasantness, sexual desire, and warmth/ love to form a cluster and excluded friendship/ fellowship from it. For females, the more a touch was associated with sexual desire the less it was considered to mean playfulness, warmth/love, friendship/fellowship, and pleasantness. The male, on the other hand, when touched in ways that indicated sexual desire, interpreted that to be more warm, more loving, and more pleasant. Tests show that these differences could not be attributed to physical differences in skin responsiveness to pressure or spatial sensitivity. The pectoral (breast) and genital areas received relatively low playfulness ratings no matter how they were touched, while all modes of touch to the hands were seen as pleasant and were given high ratings of pleasantness, warmth/love, and friendship/fellowship. Women were more discriminating regarding body location of touch, while men were more attuned to how a touch was carried out.

In a continuation study, these investigators found that with married as well as unmarried students, while there were certain resemblances there was a virtual complete reversal of their original findings on responses to the parts of the body connected with sex. The married differed considerably from the unmarried. The husbands, as compared with wives and single men, associated less pleasantness, warmth/love, and friendship with sexual touching. On the other hand the married women treated sex as highly pleasant. The authors feel that, perhaps owing to sexual liberation, contemporary American women have developed a degree of sexual interest that proves to be greater than that of their husbands. One might predict that from this failure of husbands and wives to attribute the same meanings to sexual activities, substantial problems are likely to arise—failures essentially of communication in the most intimate of marital relations.

Clearly, attitudes toward tactile communications are culturally conditioned in profound ways. Differences in marital status not only call for different roles but also result in differences in emotional response. Premaritally the American female, at least until recently, has tended to consider herself tactually sacrosanct and inviolable in areas of sexual sensitivity. The unmarried male considers her anything but so. In marriage the female tends to bloom sexually and finds sexual stimulation much more pleasant than her husband.

Trends in changes of attitude and practice toward touching during the period between 1964 and 1975 were investigated by L. B. Rosenfeld, S. Kartus, and C. Raye of the University of New Mexico. They distributed a questionnaire to 201 single men and women between ages 18 and 22. The questions related to physical contact they had had with parents and closest friends during the prior year. The results were compared with a similar study done in 1964. It appears that opposite-sex friends are today touched much more frequently and openly than in earlier years. Women touch the chest and hip regions of their male friends more frequently; men are busier touching the whole torso, from the chest down to the knees of their women friends. About 90 percent of both sexes reported that they had been touched nearly everywhere above the knees during the previous year. On the other hand, in other relationships there was little or no change. Mothers still tended to touch the sexes equally, while fathers continued to touch their daughters more than their sons. Overall the attention devoted to the body by parents and same-sex friends remained the same or increased only slightly. The investigators concluded that while opposite-sex friends may be more accessible to one another, tactile communications are no different for mothers, fathers, and same-sex friends than they were a decade ago.

Interesting sex differences in tactile response have been revealed in a study by Nicosia and Aiello of Rutgers University. They separated 80 male students into groups of four. Some were crowded shoulder to shoulder in a narrow chamber; others were jammed into a similar room but separated from each other by Plexiglass barriers. Still others were separated only by a string, while another group occupied a much larger room where each was separated by some six feet from his fellows. Eighty female students were subjected to a similar procedure. All of the subjects remained in their assigned positions for thirty minutes while the investigators observed their behavior and measured skin conductance levels as physiological indicators of anxiety. In addition to these measures the subjects' reports of their own rapid breathing, rapid heartbeats, tensing of muscles, sweating palms, and nervous tension indicated that the crowded males experienced more anxiety than the noncrowded males. The women showed much less stress than the men. The men felt most distress when forced to touch one another and found the presence of a barrier helpful. The women, however, showed increasing stress in the uncrowded situations, and the presence of barriers made them even more uneasy. They were less anxious when allowed to touch one another.

Herbert Hendin has reported that American college students are today in the midst of a revolt against intimacy. Tenderness is out, detachment is in; the emotion-free, the controlled, the invulnerable, those who have achieved maximum detachment are the most admired. The fragmentation and burial of feeling are frankly asserted as necessary and inevitable. Hence, sex is approved for the sensation but not for the feeling. One is "turned on," and inevitably one is soon "turned off." The faucet runs "hot" or "cold" at will. The less the passion involved, it seems, the better for all concerned; emotion only gets in the way. From the case studies that Hendin discusses, it is clear that the families of these students have played a major role in "turning" them off from feeling.

The damage implicit in this begins from the moment of birth, with the physical separation of the baby from the mother and the preference for bottle-feeding over breast-feeding, so long established in this century, as well as the other distancing practices characteristic of modern obstetrical and parental practices. The diversion of attention from people to things seems almost deliberate, as when mothers introduce toys into the baby's bath as a substitute for playing with the baby themselves. The child thereupon and thereafter focuses on toys rather than on people. In the home the contemporary child is surrounded by things which he alone may handle or at his discretion allows others to touch. He develops property rights in things rather than involvements with people. Moreover, as he grows he learns that adults tend to be more related to things than to each other, that they value things more than they do people, and that even the people of value to them they perceive as things and treat as such. Social distance and emotional distance become one and the same thing; relatedness to others increases as the square of the distance from them.

As the individual grows out of touch with others, he can no longer be "touched" by their suffering or their needs. Distance, magnified by the square of the television screen, lends not enchantment but ennui; in the pathological instance, which has become sufficiently common to appear ordinary, the individual is so far removed from any feeling for others that assault, rape, murder, and violence in every form loses its moral toxicity and becomes a tonic—a distraction, an amusement, and a pastime. There is no pain involved, since the violence is practiced on others. As John Carey has remarked in *The Listener*, "Art's violence is always a mirage. The most harrowing account of torture or mutilation doesn't hurt as much as someone stepping on your toe." The media and the arts have aestheticized violence, and the media especially have transformed it into an entertainment—a sensation without feeling, an aesthetic which is anesthetic. From the abandoned newborn in the antiseptic hospital crib to the highly "civilized" neutron bomb, which "only" kills people but does not disturb buildings and other nonliving things, is a gradual but entirely logical progression.

5 | LOVING: The Human Connection

Love is the supreme form of human communication. It is strange, therefore, that, while it has been the subject most celebrated in song and story, in theological and philosophical discourse, and while it has constituted the paramount principle and focal point of virtually every religion, modern scientists should nevertheless have paid so little attention to it. One might have expected at least the behavioral scientists to show some interest in the subject, but apart from the important experimental work of the Harlows on the development of love in monkeys,[1] scientists have generally refrained from treating it as a serious subject for investigation.

The reason for this is obscure. It may be that scientists have shied away from the study of love because they have considered it not quite respectable. Or it may be that, because of the constricting effects of specialization and the detaching effects of experimentation, they have simply not encountered the subject within a context congenial to wonder and exploration. Falling in love is, apparently, not a condition which encourages scientific examination of itself.

Psychoanalytic writers such as Freud, Theodore Reik, Wilhelm Reich, Ian Suttie, Rollo May, Erich Fromm, Helene Deutsch, and other writers such as Denis de Rougement and Morton Hunt have all contributed to our understanding of the nature of love; but the most significant contribution has been made by the students of the prenatal period, the birth process, the interaction between baby and mother, and their reciprocal development. Here the names of Anna Freud, John Bowlby, René Spitz, Sylvia Brody, Abraham Maslow, Sybille Escalona, Eric Erikson, Marshall Klaus, John Kennel, Berry Brazelton, Sheila Kitzinger, and Doris Haire are among the most prominent. Innumerable researchers whose names are perhaps not as well known have contributed equally to our knowledge of the nature of love. What follows is largely a distillate of these workers' findings.[2]

THE BASIC NEEDS

Fundamental to any grasp of the meaning of love is an understanding of the nature of the basic needs.

The basic needs are so called because they must be satisfied if the organism is to survive physically. They are the needs for oxygen, food, liquid, sleep, rest, activity, bowel and bladder elimination, and avoidance of painful and noxious stimuli. Physical survival is, of course, fundamental, but clearly physical survival is not what creates human beings. It is a condition for humanity only in the sense that *Homo sapiens* is born with powerful drives directed toward the realization of that humanity. Those powerful drives constitute the harmonizing need for love—not merely to *be* loved but to give love. In the hierarchy of needs, love stands as the supreme developing agent of the humanity of the person. In its relation to the other needs love may be likened to the role of the sun in our solar system: it stands at the center around which the other needs revolve, like the planets in their orbits. This analogy was beautifully expressed by George Chapman (1559?–1634), playwright and friend of Shakespeare and Ben Jonson, in his play *All Fooles*, acted in 1599, in which he makes Valerio utter these words:

> I tell thee Love is Nature's second sun,
> Causing a spring of virtues where he shines;
> And as without the sun, the world's great eye,
> All colours, beauties, both of Art and Nature,
> Are given in vain to men, so without love
> All beauties bred in women are in vain;
> All virtues born in men lie buried,
> For love informs them as the sun doth colours,
> And as the sun, reflecting his warm beams
> Against the earth, begets all fruits and flowers;
> So love, fair shining in the inward man,
> Brings forth in him the honourable fruits
> Of valour, wit, virtue, and haughty thoughts,
> Brave resolution, and divine discourse.
>
> *Act I, sc. i*

No one had ever before, nor has anyone since, captured the essence of love in such peerless words as those written by George Chapman four hundred years ago. And, as we shall see, every statement in that magnificent speech is validated by modern research.

In a very profound sense love is the most basic of all the needs, for love is the nutriment from which both physical and mental health draw their strength.

THE BIOLOGY OF LOVE

The biology of love is quite fascinating and deserves a treatise in itself. Here we can deal only with the bare outlines of the subject. Let us first consider the physical effects of love on growth and development. As often proves to be the case, it has been the observation of certain pathological conditions that has thrown the most significant light on the nature of love.

During the nineteenth century more than half the infants in their first year of life regularly died from a disease called *marasmus*, a Greek word meaning "wasting away." The disease was also known as "infantile atrophy or debility." No one had the least idea what caused the disease, but since, as Goethe pointed out, where an idea is wanting a word can always be found to take its place, so "marasmus" or "infantile debility" served to cover ignorance and to impede any genuine desire to discover the etiology of the disease. As late as the second decade of the twentieth century the death rate for infants under one year in various foundling institutions throughout the United States was nearly 100 percent. It was in 1915 that Dr. Henry Dwight Chapin, the distinguished New York pediatrician, reporting on children's institutions in ten different American cities, made the staggering disclosure that in all but one institution every infant under two years of age died. The various discussants of Dr. Chapin's report, at the Philadelphia meeting of the American Pediatric Society, fully corroborated his findings from their own experience. Dr. R. Hamil remarked, with grim irony: "I had the honor to be connected with an institution in this city of Philadelphia in which the mortality among infants under one year of age, when admitted to the institution and retained there for any length of time, was 100 percent." Dr. R. T. Southworth added, "I can give an instance from an institution in New York City that no longer exists in which, on account of the very considerable mortality among the infants admitted, it was customary to enter the condition of every infant on the admission card as hopeless. That covered all subsequent happenings." Finally, Dr. J. H. M. Knox described a study he had made in Baltimore. Of two hundred infants admitted to various institutions, almost 90 percent had died within a year. The 10 percent that survived, he stated, did so apparently because they were taken from the institutions for short periods of time and placed in the care of foster parents or relatives.

Perceiving the emotional aridity of children's institutions, Dr. Chapin introduced the system of boarding out babies instead of leaving them in the charnel houses the institutions had become. It was, however, Dr. Fritz Talbot of Boston who brought the idea of loving back with him from Germany, where he had visited before World War I. While in

Germany Dr. Talbot had called at the Children's Clinic in Düsseldorf and was shown over the wards by the director, Dr. Arthur Schlossmann. The wards were very neat and tidy, but what piqued Dr. Talbot's curiosity was the sight of a fat old lady who was carrying a baby on her hip. "Who's that?" inquired Dr. Talbot. "Oh, that," said Dr. Schlossmann, "is Old Anna. When we have done everything medically we can for a baby, and it is still not doing well, we turn it over to Old Anna, and she is always successful."

In the late 1920s, several hospital pediatricians began to introduce a regular regimen of mothering in their wards. Dr. J. Brennemann, who for a time had attended an old-fashioned foundling home where the mortality was nearer 100 percent than 50 percent, established the rule in his hospital that every baby should be picked up, carried around, and "mothered" several times a day. At Bellevue Hospital in New York, following the institution of "mothering" on the pediatric wards, the mortality rates for infants fell from 55 percent to less than 10 percent by 1938.

In short, it was discovered that infants need something more than the satisfaction of their physical basic needs if they are to make any progress—that is, to survive and grow and develop in physical and mental health. That "something" came to be recognized as what was later called "Tender, Loving Care."

In a series of studies on institutional children, beginning in 1943, Dr. William Goldfarb showed how devastatingly the personality development of such children was affected. Commencing in 1945, Dr. René Spitz, in a highly influential series of publications detailing what was in effect an unpremeditated experimental situation, demonstrated how unloved children in an institution failed on all developmental parameters as compared with institutionalized children who were loved. The infants were studied during their first year of life in two different institutions in Mexico. These places were well organized in all physical respects: in housing, asepsis, food, and hygiene. Infants were admitted to each shortly after birth. The institutions differed in but one factor: the amount of emotional interchange offered. In the first institution, called "Nursery," the infants were looked after by their own mothers. In the second institution, called "Foundlinghome," the children were raised from the third month by overworked nursing personnel, one nurse caring for from eight to twelve children. The absence or presence of emotional interchange between mother and child formed the one independent variable in the composition of the two groups.

The response to this variable, the absence or presence of "mothering," showed up in many ways but perhaps most comprehensively in the developmental quotient, which represents a measure of the total development of six sectors of the personality: mastery of perception, of bodily functions, of social relations, of memory and imitation, of manipulative ability, and of intelligence. Toward the end of the first year, although the "Foundlinghome" infants had started with a developmental quotient of 104.5 and "Nursery" infants with 101.5, the deprived "Foundlinghome" infants dropped to 72, while the "Nursery" infants rose to 105. By the end of the second year the D.Q. had fallen in the "Foundlinghome" group to the desolate low of 45, which corresponds to a developmental age of ten months.

The mortality rates in the two institutions were striking. During five years of observation involving 239 children who had been institutionalized for one year or more, "Nursery" did not lose a single child through death, whereas in "Foundlinghome" 37 percent of the children died during a two-year observation period. Death, as Spitz remarked, is but an extreme consequence of general physical and psychological decline, which affects children completely starved of emotional interchange. They die from the privation of love, just as if they had been deprived of food and died of hunger—for what they indeed die of is an unsatisfied hunger for love.

The work of John Bowlby on the psychologically disordering results of maternal deprivation and of James Robertson on the similarly deleterious effects on children of being hospitalized and separated from their mothers—a condition for which Robertson originated the term "Hospitalism"—the research of Harry Harlow and his collaborators on the behaviorally devastating effects of maternal deprivation on rhesus monkeys, and the findings of many other investigators both on humans and on a large variety of animals abundantly testify to the critical importance of love for the healthy growth and development of the individual. Characteristically the deprived individuals suffer from an inability to communicate with others at virtually all levels, social, sexual, and non-verbally. Many cases have been reported of stunted physical growth of children, a condition which has been entirely due to a lacklove experience in infancy and childhood. Often it is accompanied by varying degrees of mental retardation. It was formerly customary to attribute such cases to some physical, constitutional, or genetic deficiency. A case in point is the condition diagnosed in some children as idiopathic hypopituitarism. This term refers to the condition of dwarfism, sometimes accompanied by mental retardation, due to insufficient secretion of the growth hormone by the pituitary gland. It is now known that far from being "idiopathic" (spontaneously pathological), many such conditions are due to nothing more nor less than a lacklove environment. It has been found that children require the stimulation of affection (i.e., of love) through the senses, especially those of touch, sight, and sound, for the brain (cortex, thalamus, and hypothalamus) to transmit the necessary communications to the pituitary gland. When such stimulation is not received, and especially when it is massively withheld, there is a failure of the normally responding organs to function adequately. When one improves the emotional environment of such children the change is quite spectacular, for they commence to grow quite rapidly both physically and mentally. In some cases deprivation dwarfism may be produced by the alarm-reaction system of the body or the sympathetico-adrenal axis. The brain of the deprived child may send stress signals to the pituitary, which responds by secreting the adrenocorticotropic hormone (ACTH). This in turn stimulates the adrenal gland to secrete cortisone, a hormone which, among other things, accelerates the flow of blood to the heart. But one of the effects of cortisone on developing bone is to inhibit the proliferation of cells (fibroblasts), which are involved in the formation of new fibrous tissue, and also to produce changes in the albuminoids or collagen fibers that are so important in the formation of bone.

The evidence is now compelling that emotionally deprived animals, including humans, are less resistant to stress effects and to disease than emotionally satisfied animals, that they have higher morbidity and mortality rates, and that they tend to be less grown and developed physically and behaviorally. Loneliness in adults, which is essentially equivalent to privation of love in children, has its own damaging effects.

BEHAVIORAL EFFECTS

It is well established today that the absence of the experience of love in infancy can have the most disastrous behavioral effects. This is especially true of the ability to love and to relate to other people. It is now clear that the only way in which one ever learns to love is by being loved, that the only way one learns to relate to other people is to be warmly related to during one's infancy and early childhood.

The communications that occur between the mother and her nursing child are of the first order of importance for the subsequent healthy development of the child. By "health" is meant the ability to love, to work, to play, and to use one's mind critically. It is fundamentally important to understand these simple statements. Studies on a large variety of animals and on humans show that maternal deprivation in infancy will usually produce unloving personalities and failure in the ability to relate to others.

What, then, is love?

A succinct definition of love is that it is the ability, by demonstrative acts, to confer survival benefits on others in a creatively enlarging manner. This means that by one's acts one not only enables the other to live but to live more fully realized than he would otherwise have been.

In the absence of the criteria we have set out for loving behavior, love does not exist. In an unloving world in which there is only too often an absence of love behind the *show* of love, in which untold numbers of humans have been unloved to death or disorganization, it is particularly necessary to understand this. Unfortunately it is especially the case in the Western world and of the idolaters of Christian love—the churchgoers who all too frequently are the most unloving, ungiving, and unforgiving of humans.

What we wish to suggest is that the basic needs constitute an inbuilt value system of the individual. A value is whatever the organism considers desirable (or undesirable), the judgment of the quality of an experience. It is evident that the organism strives from the very beginning toward growth and development as a behaviorally healthy being and that it values behavioral and physical health beyond all else. Such healthy development is maximized when the organism is loved; it is more or less seriously deranged and deformed when in its earliest years it is unloved. This is quite explicitly revealed from fetal life onward. The fetus reacts to noxious stimuli with obvious distress and to the pleasurable ones (sugar in the amniotic fluid, soothing music, stroking) with obvious enjoyment. Our judgment of "obviousness" is determined by the manner in which the fetus gulps the sugar which has been introduced into the mother's amniotic fluid, by the experiences of various mothers exposed to various forms of sound, and through the soothing of hyperactive fetuses by gentle stroking of the mother's abdomen.

At every developmental stage—fetal, newborn, infant, child, adolescent, and adult—the individual shows pleasure when his basic needs are satisfied and physical and mental distress when they are not. These are the facts, and they are the facts that tell us what the organism is fundamentally *for*. They tell us that the organism is characterized by a directiveness which is oriented toward fulfillment of all its potentialities, physical and mental, for healthy growth and development.

The *facts* of human growth and development tell us in what ways the human being *ought* to grow and develop, and the inner requisites of the organism, the basic needs, clearly orient us in the direction of those satisfactions that will best meet their demands. In a much neglected but important book, *The Design of Human Behavior* (1953) by the philosopher L. A. Katsoff, these ideas (which were arrived at quite independently of the writers of the present volume) are expressed this way:

If a value is that toward which the individual directs his behavior, and positive values are those goals which are conducive to the health of the individual, then we have a meaningful and effective basis for the "ought." A positive value is one which ought to be encouraged or aimed at, its authority deriving from its relation to the health of the individual. The sanction for violating such a value is ill health—a punishment guaranteed in the sense that it will inevitably follow. So we can declare that an individual ought to strive for that which is conducive to health, though he may not do so. If he does not, we then can say that he is doing what he ought not to do.

The concept of the "ought," like the concept of value . . . has its basis in the very structure of the organism. It is, therefore, an absolute basis for any ethics or for any theory of values.

It is, of course, clear that the basic needs are not logical inferences but factual phenomena; they *ought* to be satisfied if the organism is to survive and develop, and that *oughtness* is as much a fact and lies as much in the world of *is* as do the basic needs themselves. "Ought" is in this case merely a way of denoting a necessary response—which, again, falls within the world of *is*. As Arnold Brecht so well put it, "Thus it is a factual statement rather than a logical inference when we say that feeling some specific requiredness as an *ought* is part of our human equipment. This urge, this demand, this *ought*, whatever its value and validity, is a factum, a datum, found in the world of *is*. It would be so even if only a part of mankind felt this *ought* as such. Here is the bridge, between *is* and *ought*." The nature of the basic needs conditions the oughtness of the responses; what ought to be is what the basic needs indicate, and what they indicate we are now for the first time able to decipher. In the nature of the basic needs we have the Rosetta Stone which translates for us into the vernacular what the direction of human development ought to be, what, indeed, it must be if the human species is to survive.

It has been largely due to the lack of the kind of knowledge that we have been discussing in this chapter that philosophers have claimed that there exists an unbridgeable gap between the world of fact and the world of value. We suggest that the alleged unbridgeability is due not to a gap that exists in the nature of things but to a gap that exists in the knowledge of those who generally deliver themselves on these matters. What the facts of human development, and this includes human evolution, tell us is that beyond all else human beings are born to live as if to live and love were one. This is no longer a matter merely for Sunday-morning sermons but is perfectly sound biology.

Love will always remain a matter of such fundamental importance, and will have such far-reaching consequences for humanity and society, that we are urgently called upon to consider what we can best do to restore its birthright to humanity.

To bring about the desired changes we can begin most profitably with ourselves. No matter what, then, our early environments may have been, that does not for a moment relieve us of the responsibility of making ourselves over into what we ought to be. And what ought we to be? Warm, loving human beings. The best way to bring such a condition about is to begin acting like warm, loving human beings, for what one *is* is what one *does*, not what one says or believes. If we act the role of loving beings long enough, following the guidepoints in this description of love, then we may one day awaken to find that we have become in fact what we have been enacting toward others.

The family should be the principal locus in which to apply one's love, for the only way in which children learn to love is by being loved. The school should be reperceived and reconstituted as an agency, second only in importance to the home—and sometimes superior to it—for the teaching of the science and art of love: the *science* in order to demonstrate the verifiable evidence on which the *art*—that is, the practice—of love should be based. At the college and university level such teaching should be continued and enlarged, and as in the schools all other teaching should be considered secondary to this main purpose. What passes in our schools for "education" needs to undergo a fundamental revision if we are ever to achieve the understanding and the ability to love which are so necessary for functioning as a healthy human being.

The principal qualification for a teacher, as for a parent, should be the ability to love. Just as one learns to love from being loved by one's parents, so one grows and develops in that skill under the influence of a loving teacher. And so the child grows and develops in all those other skills which he will learn best in an environment of positive reinforcement provided by the loving teacher. It was Goethe who remarked that one never learns truly to understand anything but what one loves, and in no other connection is this more true than in the understanding of children. "Without love," wrote that most wonderful of all teachers of children, Heinrich Pestalozzi, "neither the physical nor the intellectual powers of the child will develop naturally. That is only human." The greatest gift that the teacher has to bestow upon his pupils is his own personality, for when all else is forgotten, that is what will be remembered.

It is literally what the child absorbs from its teachers, as well as from its parents, that constitutes the most important influences in the making of a personality, in the acquisition of all those skills one requires for functioning well as a member of one's society and of fulfilling to the optimum one's uniquenesses, one's potentialities, for being what one has it in one creatively to be. Parents and teachers should complement each other for the benefit of everyone involved, in ministering to the needs of the child. In practical terms this means that parents and teachers should meet on a more or less regular basis in order to help each other to help their children.

The human connection begins with connecting humanly not only with other people but with whatever one experiences in school. Humanity is, surely, the central referent, and every school subject, however remote it may seem, should be taught in such a way that makes clear its relatedness to humanity, its contribution to our capacity to relate harmoniously not only to each other but to the whole of animate and inanimate nature. What could be more interesting, more exciting, more pleasurable than learning under such conditions?

The central core of every school curriculum should be the teaching of love—with all other subjects growing naturally out of such teaching.

The best way, as we see it, of carrying out such teaching is by showing how all living cells arise from other living cells and by cooperation develop into cooperating organisms; that such organisms develop (evolve) over the course of time in adaptation to the challenges of the environment by making the efficient responses; that every species grows and develops and survives cooperatively; and that the basic pattern and patent of relations between the members of each species and especially the human species is the behavior that a loving mother exhibits toward her infant. The discussion of the details involved in the teaching of the facts relating to the development of life, and especially of human life, leads naturally into the teaching of virtually every subject under the sun and most that are not taught in schools today at all.

In this way the pupil will acquire a great deal of knowledge not only about how human beings came to be what they now are but also what they ought to be now and in the future. We may not by this means achieve the millenium of total harmony in ourselves and for others, but at any rate we will be able to approach it significantly more closely than we have by our miscalled "educational" system today.

THE "FORMS" OF LOVE

There is only one form of love, although there are many descriptive varieties, known by as many names. For the Western tradition they are *Agape*, the love of God or the love of Christians for one another; *Eros*, or passionate emotion; *philia*, dutiful or filial affection; and *sex*, the sharing of emotions, feelings, fantasies, caresses, and tendernesses in sexual interaction.

What, then, is the difference between *Eros* and *sex*? There should be none, but the difference has become considerable, and that is why they are here distinguished as two different forms of "love." Unfortunately today the words for "sex" have taken the name of "love" and in a devastatingly large number of cases have replaced it. Rollo May has called this the banalization of love and sex. As he says in his book *Love and Will*, "By anesthetizing feeling in order to perform better, by employing sex as a tool to prove prowess and identity, by using sensuality to hide sensitivity, we have emasculated sex and left it vapid and empty."

"Let's make love" is the contemporary metaphor for "Let's have sex." Love frequently has not the slightest component or representation in such a proposition but represents a demand for purely physical gratification. One gets "turned on," turned over, and turned into an object; and this passes for love. The divorce rate in the United States, which now approaches one out of two marriages, merely reflects the consequence of marriages contracted on the basis of a physical attraction that most of the victims mistake to be love.

"Falling" in love is properly so called, because in addition to descending from a higher to a lower plane it generally refers to the most elementary of physical attractions. One investigator has found that the average American male thinks of sex about 75 percent of the time during the day. In other words, he appears to suffer from a chronic sexual itch. Many males recognize this for what it is, but even they seem finally to settle for a more or less permanent arrangement yielding long-term satisfactions of that itch—which is called marriage. And, of course, everyone marries for "love," although evidently most marriages are marriages of convenience, having little or nothing to do with genuine love.

In an age of confused communications it is more than ever necessary to recognize and distinguish between love and sex, to recognize that they have become very different and distinctive forms of behavior which have no necessary relation to each other. Maturity in a woman, it has been said, is achieved when she is able to distinguish between a proposal and a proposition. Since the average male is dedicated to the proposition, one might have thought that the recognition of the difference would not be difficult; but it is a measure of the failure of our culture that it has not succeeded in endowing our young with the ability to make the necessary discriminations. Such an ability comes not from attending courses on sex education but from growth and development as a warm, loving human being, with an involvement in and a consciousness of one's responsibilities to the other.

Contrary to common belief, sex is neither an instinct nor a basic need. It is a very strong drive, but it is not one that has to be satisfied if the organism is to survive, such as the needs for oxygen, liquid, food, sleep, activity, bowel and bladder elimination, and the like. Nor does sex constitute a fixed action pattern which upon the appropriate stimulus unfolds in a stereotyped reaction. Sex is something one must, for the most part, learn. The anatomical and physiological equipment is all there, but how to behave about it is something that one must acquire from experience, through learning. Unfortunately, most people, especially males, remain terribly confused about sex all their lives. Their confusion revolves about the identification of sex with love.

The Church by repressing any and all concern with sex has succeeded in making it an obsession. While the ecclesiastical and biological views of sex have much in common—namely, as principally serving the ends of reproduction—this has not been the view that most people have taken of sex. The principal purpose of sex for most people has been the pleasure it gives. But such pleasure was, and for many people still remains, even in marriage, a sin. In the Victorian period one performed "marital duties," and the subject was not discussed at all in conformity with the general Victorian principle which solved all problems quite simply by pretending that they were not there. We are only now beginning to emerge from the unctuous mean-mindedness of that hypocritical period, although the virtual disappearance of all restraints on the discussion and practice of sex has not substantially served to reduce the confusion between love and sex.

Love is not based on self-interest but on the interest of the other. This alone at once distinguishes it from so much that passes for love, and also from sex, for sex is self-interested. Where love exists, sex becomes a part of it and is enriched by it. Where sexual interest alone exists and is identified with love, love is not really there. Love and sex as communicative acts may differ from each other as the poles apart or complement each other in a consummation of one of the supreme acts of communication between two human beings.

The spurious conceptions of love are many. Probably the most widespread conception of love is that it is a commodity, something with which one bargains, as pointed out by Erich Fromm and Rollo May. As May puts it, "love" is simply the name for the way in which more powerful members of the family control other members. "Love" is made conditional on "good" behavior. The one thing that should be wholly unconditional, their "love" for the child, is made conditional on the child's obedience to the parents' will. Conditional love has given rise to what Fromm has called the "marketing" approach to love—an approach that is fully exploited by the advertising profession. "Love" is traded for "good" behavior and withheld for "bad." Children so conditioned grow up to be merchandisers in "love" both in the premarital and marital periods of their lives.

Love is the highest, profoundest, and most meaningful of the forms of communication. It is the very nexus of the human connection. It is essentially demonstrative. It is the act of communicating to others one's profound involvement in their welfare, one's devotion to the optimum fulfillment of their potentialities, by giving them all the sustenance, stimulation, and support they require for growth and development: the communication that one will never commit the supreme treason of letting them down when they most stand in need of you but that they can depend on you always to be standing by ministering to their needs, the most important of which is the need for *receiving* such communications, so that by this means they learn to be to others what you are being to them—a warm, loving human being.

If one can be these things toward other humans, then one can be said to love them. It should be observed that the description we have given of love is in all respects the manner in which a loving mother behaves toward her dependent infant. It is, in fact, the loving mother who holds the basic psychological patent on human love and who provides the crucial human pattern for every form of love.

6 | COMMUNING: The Way of Dialogue

On the far side of the subjective, on this side of the objective, on the narrow ridge, where I and Thou meet, there is the realm of "between."

—*Martin Buber*

A human being is not a black box with one orifice for emitting a chunk of stuff called communication *and another for receiving it. And, at the same time, communication is not simply the sum of the bits of information which pass between two people in a given period of time.*

—*Ray L. Birdwhistell*

The model of man which has been peculiarly congenial to the modern mind, for upward of four centuries, has been that of the machine. The interior specifications of the model have, of course, altered and improved over time—just as have machines themselves. But from the rudimentary "black box" of the seventeenth century—the Model-T of human engineering—to the contemporary cybernetic model, with its intricate network of flashing lights and whirring tapes, the portrait of Mechanical Man has remained essentially the same. It is that of an object

in nature, a stimulus-response mechanism—
indefinitely malleable, predictable, and controllable.
In the words of the father of behaviorism, John B.
Watson, man is "an assembled organic machine,
ready to run."

The mechanical model of man has, inevitably,
had its counterpart in the study of human communication, where the conventional image of the process
has been patently based on the wireless telegraph.
The key terms have been such as "sender," "re-
ceiver," "message," "transmission," "encoding," and
"decoding." In the new age of computers, as communication theory has given way to information
theory, the metaphors have been correspondingly
updated; now the operative terminology includes
"feedback," "input-output-throughput," "bits,"
"noise," etc. Not only is the image of the machine
still prevalent in the cybernetic era; it is more trium-
phant than ever. In fact the advent of the computer
has made possible an entire new universe of discourse: communication between machine and machine, as well as between machine and man. Thus
the equation of the human and the mechanical has
been profoundly reinforced. Whereas in the older
approach human communication was hypothetically
modeled in the image of the machine, now there are
actual "communication machines" out there which
have been created in the image of the human—
playing human games, practicing human therapy,
writing human prose, and impersonating human
speech. Not long ago, for an anxious moment, it
seemed as if nothing human was alien to them; and
there have even been some who speculated that, by

the year 2001 if not sooner, they would not only be doing our "communication" better but controlling it as well.

However, as early as the 1950s, the mechanical model began to exhibit signs of obsolescence—even of irrelevance. In retrospect, it seems likely that the turning point occurred with the publication (and public impact) of Norbert Wiener's *The Human Use of Human Beings*. Here was the father of cybernetics himself proclaiming in apocalyptic terms ("The hour is very late, and the choice of good and evil knocks at our door") that the application of communication machines to the solution of human problems constitutes an abuse of machines and an inhuman use of human beings. It was not, of course, that Wiener was prophesying a science-fictive Armageddon, with computers in the saddle riding mankind; his warning rather was against the tendency, and the temptation, to abandon human modes of thought and discourse in favor of "thinking like machines"—and thereby making a self-fulfilling prophecy out of the mechanical model of communication.

Any machine constructed for the purpose of making decisions, if it does not possess the power of learning, will be completely literal-minded. Woe to us if we let it decide our conduct, unless we have previously examined the laws of its action, and know fully that its conduct will be carried out on principles acceptable to us! On the other hand, the machine like the djinnee, which can learn and can make decisions on the basis of its learning, will in no way be obliged to make such decisions as we should have made, or will be acceptable to us. For the man who is not aware of this, to throw the problem of his responsi-

bility on the machine, whether it can learn or not, is to
cast his responsibility to the winds, and to find it coming
back seated on the whirlwind.[1]

At first it appeared that Wiener's was a voice cry-
ing in the wilderness. But it was soon echoed by
other voices from other rooms, which took on the
proportions of a chorus (indeed, an accusing Greek
chorus). The common theme was clear and unmistakable: the mode of discourse, and of thought, appropriate to machines is inappropriate to human beings. We are not machines, nor were we meant to be;
we can be reduced to the level of mechanism only by
surrendering to its mystique and blindly going
through its motions. In part because of the dilemmas
posed by scientific humanists like Wiener, and perhaps in larger part because of critical confrontations
in the real world (both international and countercul-
tural), there has grown up in recent years a new
realization that there are indeed two modes of discourse which stand in mutual opposition—those
which Anatol Rapoport has referred to as the com-
peting voices of "strategy and conscience." In sim-
pler terms, they are the modes of *monologue* and
dialogue. The conflict between them is ancient and
chronic; it has also been generally one-sided, since
the monological mode serves the ends of *power* while
the dialogical mode serves only the ends of *community*. The prototype of the monologue is one person
talking at another; the prototype of the dialogue is
two persons talking with each other. To be sure, the
difference between the two modes is not always so
obvious; much of what passes for dialogue, as in

ordinary conversation, is in reality a series of alternating monologues. Indeed it is in the interest of monologue, since its end is persuasion and its usual means ingratiation, to wrap itself in the mantle of dialogue. Sometimes this disguise is easily enough penetrated; we are all familiar with the experience related by Joost Meerloo and would presumably agree with his conclusion:

I cannot converse with my authoritarian-minded friend. His looks are too serious and he dictates the subject matter at dinner. The play of conversation must be a collective action; it must be speaking in such a way that the listener is able to receive the words and to know how to deal with them. It must remain a mutual experience, for only so is it real communication.[2]

Since a common attribute of the monological mode is deception (including self-deception), and because of the general tendency in everyday encounters to take the appearance for the reality (what Goffman calls "trust"), it is often difficult to recognize the true nature of a verbal transaction or conversational exchange. Even experience is not an infallible guide. We are recurrently beguiled by the confidential manner of the salesman, a total stranger until only a moment ago, who calls us by our first name and places an affectionate hand on our shoulder as he guides us (eyes glazed and wings folded) into his web. "Would I lie to you?" he asks, looking us straight in the eye; and we are immediately ashamed of our lack of trust.

The preeminent philosopher of dialogue, Martin Buber, has dealt at length with the subtle distinctions, in form as well as essence, which separate the genuine from the spurious—the authentic from the unauthentic—in the contingent world of interpersonal communication. He has identified three different kinds of "dialogue," only one of which is the real thing. "There is *genuine dialogue*—no matter whether spoken or silent—where each of the participants really has in mind the other or others in their present and particular being and turns to them with the intention of establishing a living mutual relation between himself and them." This kind of dialogue, according to Buber, has become rare in the modern world; perhaps it was always rare, for it requires a heightened capacity for *giving*—what a Freudian might call the suspension of the ego—as well as a willingness (familiar in Eastern thought but not in Western practice) to "let be." Wherever this infrequent kind of dialogue does arise, says Buber, "witness is borne on behalf of the continuance of the organic structure of the human spirit."

The second form is dealt with summarily as "technical dialogue, which is prompted solely by the need of objective understanding." Buber might well have lingered on this topic, since the category would appear to embrace virtually the entire field covered by conventional communication theory—that is, the reciprocal exchange of information. It is enough for present purposes to observe that, for Buber, this is "dialogue" only in an entirely technical sense: it involves an exchange, and it has an objective content. To be sure, there is a superficial authenticity, or at least a kind of integrity, to this technical form of communication, so long as it does not pretend to be other than it is—namely, monologue in its "pure" form, stripped of persuasive overtones or manipulative undertones. It might be added that, just as genuine dialogue has become a rare occurrence, so has pure monologue become a rare commodity in the contemporary world of commerce, advertising, and everyday "public relations."

Buber's delineation of the third kind of supposed dialogue is that of "monologue disguised as dialogue, in which two or more men, meeting in space, speak each with himself in strangely tortuous and circuitous ways and yet imagine they have escaped the torment of being thrown back on their own resources." This anomalous yet common situation, in which there is an appearance of what might be termed "sincere insincerity," is reminiscent of the existentialist treatment of "bad faith" (*mauvais foi*)—the "lie in the soul" which is hidden even from the liar. As Buber describes it, this it the most common of failings in the realm of dialogue—embracing such diverse encounters as a *debate*, "in which the thoughts are not expressed in the way in which they existed in the mind but in the speaking are so pointed that they may strike home in the sharpest way," with at the same time a total indifference to the presence of the other debaters as persons; a *conversation* which is "characterized by the need neither to communicate something, nor to learn something, nor to influence someone, nor to come into connexion with someone, but solely by the desire to have one's self-reliance confirmed by marking the impression that is made"; a *friendly chat* "in which each regards himself as absolute and legitimate and the other as relativized and questionable"; and, finally, a *lovers' talk*, or rather that version of it "in which both partners alike enjoy their own glorious soul and their precious experience." Terminating his list with a flourish, Buber exclaims: "What an underworld of faceless spectres of dialogue!"

Nevertheless it is possible, if only at rare moments or for rare persons, to escape that underworld and enter the realm of authentic dialogue—replacing the faceless specters with real faces and embodied presences. "The basic movement of the life of dialogue," says Buber, "is the turn towards the other." Dialogue occurs when, out of all the manipulated and manipulating objects in the human world, one discovers a subject: the *I* creates a *Thou*. ". . . out of the incomprehensibility of what lies to hand this one person steps forth and becomes a presence." Then there is genuine meeting—not only mutual recognition but mutual confirmation. And something more: an attitude toward fellow human beings, however fleeting and infrequent, which bears no trace of opportunism or exploitation—which perceives in the human parade not a crowd nor a "mass" nor even an audience but a collection of individuals each one of whom, without exception, can be recognized as a person. To confirm the other in this way, in his full humanity, carries with it the unexpected blessing: oneself is confirmed in turn.

ROLE-TAKING VS. ROLE-PLAYING

Buber's image of the basic movement of dialogue— the turn toward the other—has its (somewhat more prosaic) counterpart in the sociological concept of role-taking, associated with the school of thought known as symbolic interactionism and first given prominence in the classic work of George Herbert Mead. Role-taking is not to be understood as the playing of parts or the putting on of masks; rather it means simply adopting the standpoint of the other in communication, assimilating his perspective in order to apprehend his meanings and anticipate his actions. In its original version, this conception of "role" had no theatrical overtones or manipulative connotations; on the contrary it expressed a sense of common kinship in symbolic interaction, a capacity for mutual understanding and hence for mutual regard.

But, at the hands of later students of interaction, role-taking began to give way to role-playing—with the emphasis less on mutual comprehension than on mutual manipulation. Recent research has typically taken the form of case studies aimed at penetrating the ingenious ways through which persons in various circumstances manage the contingencies, juggle the variables, grasp at opportunities, and generally maneuver for advantage. Perhaps the most impressive and influential exemplar of what might be called the new interactionism is Erving Goffman (a graduate of the "Chicago school" founded by Mead), whose work we have sampled copiously in earlier chapters. Goffman's first book, *The Presentation of Self in Everyday Life*, is a richly embellished and gracefully constructed portrayal of the strategies and styles employed by "Everyman" in the process (no longer viewed as simple) of getting through the day. This daily test of skill, and ordeal of endurance, is depicted as a series of self-presentations through which the individual seeks not only to put his best face forward (the "expressions that he gives") but also to manage and control the responses of others (the "impressions that he gives off"). In this book, as in his later work, Goffman demonstrated as no one had done before the *problematic* character of everyday life: the delicate negotiations, elaborate rituals, and subtle communications between persons which are essential to bringing off even the most routine and commonplace encounters. A sample of Goffman's explanatory prose may serve to illustrate the complexity of motives and interests seen to lie beneath the smooth surface of ordinary interaction:

Let us now turn from the others to the point of view of the individual who presents himself before them. He may wish them to think highly of him, or to think that he thinks highly of them, or to perceive how in fact he feels toward them, or to obtain no clear-cut impression; he may wish to ensure sufficient harmony so that the interaction can be sustained, or to defraud, get rid of, confuse, mislead, antagonize, or insult them. Regardless of the particular objective which the individual has in mind and of his motive for having this objective, it will be in his interests to control the conduct of the others, especially their responsive treatment of him. This control is achieved largely by influencing the definition of the situation which the others come to formulate, and he can influence this definition by expressing himself in such a way as to give them the kind of impression that will lead them to act voluntarily in accordance with his own plan.[3]

As this passage suggests, there is a special nuance in the analysis of interaction conducted by Goffman and his followers—a sensitivity to the "strategic" and manipulative measures employed in the process of self-presentation which gives the activity the appearance of a contest or game. Lofland, in a critical appraisal of "interactionist imagery," has described the attitude:

Attuned as interactionists are to social life as a *constructed* product of *active* humans, a number of similar terms and styles that refer to a single stance have begun to creep into their studies and essays. Terms that denote this stance have included the following: management, strategies, tactics, devices, mechanisms, maneuvers, stratagems, practices. . . . In other words, there is here a stripped down and modest version of game theory.[4]

Goffman has often made explicit the strategic or game-playing dimension in his studies of face-to-face interaction, most systematically in a volume prefaced by the comment that it "deals with the calculative, gamelike aspects of mutual dealings—what will be called *strategic interaction.*" One section of this book is addressed to "Expression Games," in particular those situations where an observer seeks information from a subject who is either reluctant to divulge it or concerned to manage it in some way. "Under these conditions gamelike considerations develop even though very serious matters may be at stake. A contest over assessment occurs. Information becomes strategic and expression games occur." Goffman observes that in such a game of mental skill there are typical "moves" on the part of the respective players; on one side the subject may make "unwitting" or "naive" moves which betray his information, or he may attempt a "covering move" to influence the observer's interpretation; on the other side the observer, if he suspects such trickery, can perform an "uncovering move" in an attempt to "crack, pierce, penetrate, and otherwise get behind the apparent facts in order to uncover the real ones." Even that is not necessarily the end of the affair; if the subject is onto the observer's game, he may come back with a guileful move to check or undo the other—what Goffman terms the "counter-uncovering move," typically one of slyly permitting the observer to suppose that he has indeed cracked the façade, found the truth, and won the day.

In this analysis of strategic interactions, Goffman has clearly gone beyond the reference to games as a useful analogy to define the real-life encounter as itself a game—even if, at the extreme, a deadly game. (Indeed, much of the volume is taken up with an examination, in similar terms, of the undercover activity of espionage and counterespionage—surely a "game" in deadly earnest.) In his espousal of a game-theoretical approach to social interaction, at least in some of its forms, Goffman appears to have been persuaded by the sophisticated method of "strategic analysis" developed by Thomas C. Schelling, which represents an adaptation of the classic theory of games to social, political, and especially international relations. It is well to point out that strategic game theory, descended from mathematics, like the exchange theory of social relations derived from economics, is simplistically reductive in its bloodless account of the nature of human interaction; moreover, it perpetrates an ethics of "winning through intimidation" (or through exploitation or manipulation or fraud) which, however workable and worked it may be, runs directly counter to those fragile traditions of civility and tolerance that sustain a democratic society.

DRAMATIS PERSONAE

There is a further dimension in the influential work of Goffman which not only gives it distinction but makes it distinctly controversial. His first book was prefaced with the announcement: "The perspective employed in this report is that of the theatrical performance; the principles derived are dramaturgical ones." Presentations of self in everyday life are accordingly regarded as performances by "actors" defined in a new and particular way—not merely as individuals carrying out actions, as in traditional interactionism, but as players doing a part in a theatrical setting which has both "front-stage" and "backstage" regions. The front region includes the stage and set in which the performance is played out, as well as the audience before whom it is played; the backstage area is any place behind the scenes where masks may be removed and actors are no longer "on."

The distinction between front and backstage regions is illustrated by the seemingly schizoid behavior of those (for example in the service occupations) whose jobs require a public "front" that is dispensed with when they leave the "set." The prototype of the quick-change artist, one who puts on and takes off roles with ease, is of course the professional entertainer. Said Sammy Davis, Jr., "As soon as I go out the front door of my house in the morning, I'm on, Daddy, I'm on. . . . But when I'm with the group I can relax. We trust each other." (Davis's front-stage awareness, however, may have been more than the product of professionalism; as one observer noted in 1950, "Negroes in our [white] culture spend most of their lives 'on' . . . Every Negro is to some extent a performer." On the other hand, when "relaxing among themselves," blacks may "mock the 'type' personalities they are obliged to assume when they're 'on.' ")

It may be that public attitudes toward the obligatory dual personality of the entertainer or celebrity have become gradually more sophisticated, or at least more complexly confused, in a mass-mediated society in which publicity has all but obliterated privacy. Where once the career of a matinee idol (like Francis X. Bushman in the Twenties) could be instantly destroyed by the revelation that he was a husband and father—hence of mortal clay—today there is a flourishing industry of "backstage" media (evinced not only in "people" magazines but in TV talk shows and celebrity sports events) which at once depends on the separate reality and candid intimacy of backstage regions and, by its very presence there, transforms them into new front stages. The performer, caught in this double bind, must contrive to maintain two sets of illusions rather than one; he must appear to be a different person (his real self) backstage, but he cannot afford to be really "off." The candid camera will get him if he doesn't watch out.

In the process of extrapolation by sociologists of a dramaturgical bent, the analogy between real life and theatrical fiction has come to be greatly magnified and possibly overstretched. Goffman himself, while borrowing copiously from the rhetoric of stagecraft for his graphic terminology (e.g., "theatrical frame," "dramatic realization," "scripts," "performances," and so on), has generally taken pains to confine his dramaturgy to the modest status of a suggestive metaphor and even to insist that life is *not* theater, nor even entirely *like* theater. Others have gone much further, to the point of dissolving any perceptible difference between the theater of life and the life of theater. Thus Stanford Lyman and Marvin B. Scott declare: "Social reality, then, is realized theatrically. Otherwise put, reality is a drama, life is theater, and the social world is inherently dramatic."

Their argument is not, of course, that human beings in everyday life are self-consciously "play-acting," posturing, and impersonating famous men—although in childhood, at unguarded moments even in adulthood, and in extreme situations (such as in mental hospitals), they may do just that; what is maintained is that the perspective of "dramatism" is uniquely appropriate to the facts of life as lived (performed) by acting persons in existential roles. Life itself is an *agon*, a struggle or conflict carried forward through progressive "acts" and occurring in successive "scenes" (situations)—complete with climaxes and anticlimaxes, entrances and exits, supporting players ("significant others"), and audiences real and imagined. Life, in this view, is not "like" a dramatic presentation; it has the intrinsic character of unwritten drama, of improvisational theater in earnest. Our lives are such stuff as dreams are made on, and then written down as drama; the play is an imitation of life.

These recent theories of social interaction as role-playing—either as a game or as a drama—may appear to be denying our lives a dimension of integrity or even of seriousness. But they have in common a respect for the intricacy and ingenuity of our daily maneuvers through the crowded traffic—the sheer intelligence that is required, and displayed, in the process of getting through the day. The people they portray for us, the human beings who emerge from these studied vignettes, are (if nothing else) *survivors*—persons who act upon their world, who negotiate and resist, manage and make out. That may not be all that we would like to see, or believe to be happening, in the communications and contacts of daily life. But it is a beginning toward an appreciation of the uncommon sense commonly exhibited by "ordinary people" in everyday encounters.

Other social scientists of the new wave have carried this emphasis further. The school of ethnomethodology pioneered by Harold Garfinkel is especially notable for its attention to the underlying meanings of social interaction in the common-sense world—carried out by means of a form of "naturalistic observation" which respects both the standpoint and the ordinary language of the people who inhabit that world. There is an insistence on the active and conscious nature of social behavior and on the emergent character (the "contextual determination") of meaning—which is not to be deduced from a set of norms or a collection of data but must be *in*duced from a sharing of the perspectives and common-sense experience of the participants in interaction. The essential mandate is to respect the ordinary world and its inhabitants.

Closely related to, if not descended from, the school of ethnomethodology is the "sociology of everyday life"—an orientation which, under the guidance of Jack D. Douglas in particular, is anchored in *praxis* as well as in theory—that is, it seeks both to understand and to enhance the conditions of ordinary life. The starting point of this approach is, once more, the "inescapable reference-point" of the common-sense world, which is taken to be the basis of all experience and conjecture, including that of social scientists. "Once we recognize," writes Douglas, "that the phenomena of our common-sense experience are the fundamental data for any sociological ideas and theory, we look upon a world that was previously irrelevant to our work as sociologists. *We discover everyday life.*"

Such *concerned engagement* is an intrinsic (if latent) property of the commitment to a view which holds the actions of men and women to be meaningful, their minds to be conscious, their talk to be reasonable, and their lives to be worth while. They may not always be in communion; but they are indisputably in communication.

7 | DANCING: The Rhythm of Life

Dancing is the loftiest, the most moving, the most beautiful of the arts, because it is no mere translation or abstraction from life; it is life itself.

—*Havelock Ellis*, The Dance of Life

A remarkable breakthrough in the scientific study of communication has been made possible by the movie camera and projector. In brief, the camera eye has revealed a dimension of human communication that was previously hidden from view—*synchrony* or *rhythm.*

Through the investigations of leading kinesicists such as Birdwhistell, Condon, and Hall—aided by the use of sophisticated film equipment—it has been discovered that persons involved in social interaction unconsciously move "in sync" with one another through a rhythmic coordination of gestures and movements which exhibits all the characteristics of a dance. As with the "micromomentary" facial expressions described in an earlier chapter, this kinesic ballet is not perceptible when filmed episodes are shown at normal projection speeds (usually 18 or 24 frames per second) but becomes apparent at very slow speeds—as well as when the projector is stopped at successive or near successive frames for closer inspection of the tableau. Paradoxically, the rhythm of interaction may also be revealed by showing films—e.g., of family gatherings—at very fast speeds.

An early example of this phenomenon, which has become something of a classic among kinesicists, is the "Cigarette Scene" captured on film in the mid-Fifties and subsequently subjected to microscopic investigation by Birdwhistell and a group of distinguished collaborators including Gregory Bateson, Henry Broslin, Charles Hockett, Norman A. McQuown, and Frieda Fromm-Reichmann. The interactional sequence, lasting just 18 seconds, has as its manifest content a conversational exchange which is a segment of a longer interview between a woman called Doris and a visiting interviewer identified as Gregory. The action proceeds as follows:

Doris and Gregory, as the camera is reloaded and again begins to record the scene, are reseated upon the sofa. Each has a stein of the homemade beer supplied by Doris. Doris looks from Gregory to her beer stein and at the matches which Gregory is holding. Her left hand carries the cigarette to her mouth after her right leaves the stein on the coffee table before them. Gregory continues: "He's a very, very bright four-and-a-half-year-old. Why, that drawing that he brought in is very advanced for four-and-a-half." As he talks, he opens the match folder, extracts a match, strikes the match under the closed flap, moves the lighted match into position and makes contact with her cigarette as he terminates his vocalization. As he talks, Doris moves in concert with his match manipulations until her cigarette is lighted. She speaks: "I suppose all mothers think their kids are smart, but I have no worries about that child's intellectual ability." A 3/8 second lag between "child's" and "intellectual" was equaled by another between "intellectual" and "ability." Gregory speaks, his first words coterminous with the latter hesitation and "ability": "No, that's a very smart one." As Doris talks, her right hand drops to the table edge and then past it slightly to the left to adjust her shoe strap before she drops her hand backward to the couch. This movement, with its momentary shifts, are still in concert with Gregory's, who, after Doris' cigarette is lighted, forms a triangular movement in the air which terminates with the extinguishing of the match and its disposal in the ash tray.[1]

This fleeting and "trivial" episode has continued to charm and fascinate students of nonverbal communication through two decades of research, despite the accumulation of countless newer reels detailing more weighty encounters and interactions. The reason for continued interest is that the brief sequence presents a neatly rounded unit (with a beginning, middle, and end) of perfectly "timed" and coordinated movements—a highly stylized, if unconscious, *pas de deux*. Thus Birdwhistell, in analyzing the scene, refers to the "special cadence" of the interaction, the "ritual dancelike lighting" of Doris' cigarette, the "glove-fit coherence of the rhythmic movements" of the participants, which Gregory brings flourishingly to a close by "a batonlike change of pace."

The silent duet of body language, which the Cigarette Scene nicely illustrates, might seem to be a phenomenon peculiar to two-person encounters (dyads) in which there are no distractive influences or additional inputs to be accommodated. However, researchers into synchrony have found that the same rhythmic interaction—what Meerloo has termed "cooscillation"—exists in groups of widely varying size, ranging from a nuclear family unit to an entire classroom of children spilled out on a playground. While one might expect a certain amount of "harmony" and orchestration within a family group, the opposite would seem more probable—mere anarchy loosed on the world—in the case of a horde of small children scattered on a school playground at lunch hour. But this apparently disorganized event, as filmed by Edward T. Hall and his students and exhaustively reviewed, turned out to have a coherent rhythmic "arrangement," a distinctive beat, and even a "conductor."

At first, they looked like so many kids each doing his own thing. After a while, we noticed that one little girl was moving more than the rest. Careful study revealed that she covered the entire playground. . . . Gradually, [we] perceived that the whole group was moving in synchrony to a definite rhythm. The most active child, the one who moved about most, was the director, the orchestrator of the playground rhythm![2]

The silent beat of the children's play was so perceptible that an expert in rock music was able to devise a tune to match the rhythm. "Then," Hall tells us, "the music was synchronized with the children's play and once synchronized remained in sync for the entire 4½ minutes of the film clip!"
Another striking example of synchrony may be

seen in an experiment by W. S. Condon in which two persons were hooked up to an electroencephalograph while engaged in conversation, with one camera filming the principals while another focused on the machine. During the entire period of conversation, the two EEG recording pens moved in such perfect unison as to appear "driven" by a single force; only when the talk was interrupted by a third person did the readings diverge. On the basis of many such experiments over a period of some fifteen years, Condon has concluded that interaction within a culture is governed by "body synthesizers" set in motion almost immediately after birth and thereafter conditioned by culture. On this view, interpersonal communication is not a matter of "isolated entities sending discrete messages" back and forth but a process of mutual participation in a common structure of rhythmic patterns shared by all members of the culture.

While culture evidently shapes the particular tempo of kinesic and linguistic behavior, it is "nature and nurture"—the experience of infancy—which instills the rhythm of life. Research has shown that the fetus is capable of responding to sound as well as to pressure and that the beating of its own heart at about 140 beats per minute, together with the beating of its mother's heart at a frequency of 70, provides it with what has been described as a syncopated world of sound. Laved by the amniotic fluid to the symphonic beat of two hearts, the baby is already in tune with the deepest rhythms of existence. The dance of life has begun.

More than one observer has seen a connection between the sync of mother-fetus heartbeats and the rhythmic beat of music. A popular motion-picture film of the 1930s—*Zwei Herzen in Dreiviertel Takt* (*Two Hearts in Three-Quarter Time*)—graphically illustrates the point. Its title song was a waltz composed, like all waltzes, in three-quarter time: 1, 2, 3, exactly as the baby's heart beats, during most of its time *in utero*, twice for every one beat of the mother's heart. Nor does the primal waltz of mother and infant terminate at birth; it resumes whenever the baby is held on the mother's left side (a preference shared both by humans and monkeys) where the apex of the maternal heart is more exposed and the baby is able to hear the solacing rhythm of its mother's heartbeat. The cradling and rocking of the infant, as Joost Meerloo points out, duplicates the "nirvanic dance" of the fetus in the womb; so also does the "milk dance," the rhythmic interaction between mother and child during suckling at the breast. "Here is where the rhythmic behavior of the mother—rocking the cradle; singing lullabies; carrying and coddling the child; holding it 'under her heart' (in the double meaning of the word)—serves to supply and guarantee feelings of security and protected dependency."

In this behavioral field as in others, ontogeny parallels (if it does not recapitulate) phylogeny; the rhythms that begin for the individual within the womb resemble the oceanic rhythms that have reverberated in us, as Darwin supposed, from the time when the first amphibians ventured forth from the sea. "Neuropathologically," writes Meerloo, "we know that there is also a relation between rhythm and the archaic sense of vibration." Cosmic rhythms—the music of the spheres—both precede and transcend human existence; more pertinently they also support it, in part control it, and in some sense define it. As Hall summarizes: "All living things internalize and respond to dozens of rhythms—night and day, lunar, seasonal, annual, as well as the shorter cycles and rhythms such as breathing rate, heart beat, and the various brain waves—to say nothing of the rhythms of hunger and sex." In short, we all got rhythm.

There are multiple layers and levels of rhythm, within and around us, overlapping and contrapuntal. It appears, for one thing, that each of us acquires a personal beat, our own "composition" as it were, which is expressed in what we call personality. As Thoreau said, "If a man does not keep pace with his companions, perhaps it is because he hears a different drummer. Let him step to the music which he hears, however measured or far away." Underlying that individual note, nonetheless, is the insistent tempo and cadence imposed by culture, the distinctive beat of the tribal drum. And still deeper within us there resounds the ur-rhythm of life itself, the primordial pulse that provides what Meerloo has termed "the universal communion of archaic behavior."

These subterranean levels of rhythmic interaction—the biological and the cultural—represent the oldest links in the "Great Chain of Being"—the aboriginal human connection. They are the wellspring of music and the origin of dance—perhaps of all art. Moreover, they are essential ele-

ments in the sound system of man, as Peter Ostwald
has described it; for the physical properties of sonic
events are nothing other than vibrations produced
by motion. "The human auditory system is a specialized device capable of receiving these physical
results of movement and analyzing them into meaningful components. As a physical medium, sound
lends itself particularly well to ordering, sequencing,
temporal structuring, and simultaneous tonal over-
laps." The sense of rhythm, partly innate and partly
acquired, is the ordering principle—the sounding
board—which not only makes chords out of discord
but, magically and mysteriously, fashions speech
out of sputter.

Rhythm is not only infectious; it is often contagious. Where the beat is shared, the sound of music
and the movement of dance call out a response that is
automatic and all but irresistible; they may set the
feet to tapping, the hands to clapping, the fingers to
snapping. The sense we call aesthetic is at first
kinesthetic; before we can respond with our minds
we "feel it in our bones." Nor is man the only creature capable of transforming the felt rhythm of life
into the public spectacle of dance; among numerous
species, from ants to apes, there are ceremonial performances characterized by rhythmic elegance and
expressive eloquence. Here, for example, is a description given us by J. McLaren of the dance of the
stilt birds in Australia:

There were some hundreds of them and their dance was
in the manner of quadrille, but in the matter of rhythm
and grace excelling any quadrille that ever was. In

groups of a score or more they advanced and retreated, lifting high their long legs and standing on their toes, now and then bowing gracefully one to another, now and then one pair encircling with prancing daintiness a group whose heads moved upwards, downwards and sideways in time to the stepping of the pair. At times they formed into one great, prancing mass . . . then suddenly . . . they would sway apart, some of them to rise in low, encircling flight . . . ; and presently they would form in pairs or sets of pairs, and the prancing and the bowing, and advancing and retreating would begin all over again. . . .[3]

The "quadrille" of the stilt birds, like the "waltz" of the ostrich and the "minuet" of the courting dove, represent behaviors which resemble the human dance in their dependence on rhythmic coordination but which are otherwise unrelated to the mores and music of mankind. But what are we to say of the intricate and inventive round dance performed by the apes of Teneriffe, as described for us by Kohler?

. . . two of them . . . begin to circle about, using the post as a pivot. One after another the rest of the animals appear, join the circle, and finally the whole group, one behind the other, is marching in orderly fashion around the post. Now their movements change quickly. They are no longer walking but trotting. Stamping with one foot and putting the other down lightly, they beat out what approaches a distinct rhythm, with each of them tending to keep step with the rest. Sometimes they bring their heads into play and bob them up and down, with jaws loose, in time with the stamping of their feet.[4]

In this group dance, as Curt Sachs has noted, appear many of the central elements and motifs of the dance as practiced in human societies around the world and in all historical periods, among them the forward and backward pace; the pivotal forms of the circle and ellipse; the rhythmic movements of hopping, whirling, and stamping; and the use of ornamentation or "costume."

Whether or not there is any biological connection between this anthropoid activity and the dance forms of man, it is clear that there is a connection through learning—that is, through imitation and "impersonation." Animal mime dances are among the most basic, recurrent, and richly varied of dance themes in the tribal repertoire, related not only to the hunt but to totemic rites of worship and propitiation of spirits incarnated in animals. As this suggests, animal mime dances are not merely imitative but symbolic and dramatistic; they are elevated to the human level by the addition of ritual, religion, and narration. That indeed is the definitive element of all human dance; it is not merely rhythmic but expressive, and it is not only expressive but communicative. As Frances Rust, a historian of dance, reminds us, "In the life of primitive peoples, nothing approaches the dance in significance. It is no mere pastime, but a very serious activity. It is not a sin but a sacred act." The forms of the dance are as varied as the functions of the group; the meanings of the dance are as deep as the sensitivities of the race. The very life of the community—or, more accurately, its life-spirit—is transmitted and sustained through dance. According to Curt Sachs, "Birth, circumcision, and the consecration of maidens, marriage and death, planting and harvest, the celebrations of chieftains, hunting, war and feasts, the changes of the moon, and sickness—for all of these the dance is needed."

The rhythms that find expression in dancing are themselves widely varied. There are rhythms (of slow tempo, played *pianissimo*) that duplicate the maternal lullaby, inducing reverie and meditation; this is the music that hath charms to soothe the savage breast. But the tribal drum no less often sounds the alarm and calls to arms; as Meerloo observes, "there is panic in the flute of Pan." Group rituals such as chants, war dances, parades and marches, mass rallies and demonstrations quicken the pulse and stir the blood—often overwhelming the tentative note of personal identity in the drumbeat of communal co-oscillation. Then inhibition succumbs to exhibition, repression to expression, singularity to solidarity; the resonant rhythm of the group is released through such actions as singing, chanting, praying, dancing, swaying, hand-holding, and marching. When several of these forms of rhythmic expression are combined in a single group performance, the result is frequently ecstatic.

The dance of religious ecstasy—aimed at inducing a trancelike state through such exertions as drumming, whirling, jumping, and howling—is of ancient origin and appears to have been practiced in all parts of the world. In classical Greece the *Orgia* dances of the Dionysian cultists introduced the practice of sacramental intoxicants and set the pattern for cathartic orgies in the name of religious devotion. In the Moslem world the dances of the whirling (and howling) dervishes are still practiced among some thirty Islamic sects. In all ecstatic dances, as in the crazes classified under the heading of collective behavior, there is a voluntary abandonment of identity and a willing surrender to what used to be called the "group mind." The insistent rhythm has a contagious appeal and a hypnotic effect; but in most cases the results appear to be harmless to the participants if not clearly beneficial.

However, in some notorious instances the ecstatic dance has lost its exuberance, ceased to be joyful, and become compulsive and pathogenic. Such dances, in Sachs's words, are "out of harmony with the body." By an alteration of chemistry rhythm becomes dis-rhythm, control disappears, and coordination fails; what was symbolic becomes symptomatic as the frenzied dance deteriorates into convulsion, agitation, and paroxysm. Although pathogenic dances have been frequently observed by anthropologists in tribal cultures, the most massive and persistent example of the phenomenon—literally an epidemic—was that of the "dancing mania" which spread through Europe during the Middle Ages. For more than two centuries, as Rust describes it, there were periodic outbreaks of "a wild, leaping dance performed by people screaming and foaming with fury, having all the appearance of persons 'possessed.'" On one occasion, in 1374, some thousands of celebrants visiting Aachen, Germany, for a midsummer festival "suddenly began to leap and scream in the streets. Losing all control they danced for hours until overcome by exhaustion." These "manic dancers" wandered from town to town, through the Low Countries and into France, periodically resuming their frenzied gyrations; and wherever they went, the contagion of their spastic rhythm spread to spectators, who reportedly joined their ranks by the scores and hundreds. While some in this strange throng appear to have been anxious family members or sheer opportunists, most were evidently genuine if unwilling converts to the macabre revelry. And for some at least, accustomed to leading lives of quiet desperation, the episode was not without its compensations:

Peasants left their ploughs, mechanics their workshops, housewives their domestic duties, to join the wild revels. . . . Secret desires were excited and but too often found opportunities for wild enjoyment. . . . Above a hundred unmarried women were seen raving about in consecrated and unconsecrated places and the consequences were soon perceived.

It is probable, of course, that the medieval dancing mania is to be explained at least in part by physical causes. The name of "St. Vitus' Dance," associated nowadays with the disease of chorea (whose symptoms include involuntary rhythmic movements), was first given to the victims of an outbreak of the dancing mania at Strasbourg in 1418 who were taken for treatment to the chapels of St. Vitus, patron saint of the afflicted. Europe was still recovering from the devastation of the Black Death, and there was no lack of diseases "in the air" that might account for the antic behavior of the possessed dancers—notably the nervous disorder called "tarantism," supposedly brought on by the poisonous bite of the tarantula, whose victims danced compulsively in a style that gave the name to the tarantella. Even this condition, however, appears to have been induced more by fear of what the spider's bite might do than by the actual bite itself. Not only was dancing the tarantella seen as a symptom of tarantism; it was also, ironically, regarded as an efficacious remedy—on the theory that the feverish dance would bring the poison to the surface of the skin and speed its elimination. A form of dance that can be regarded simultaneously as a disease symptom and a cure—i.e., as both good and evil—must have held a powerful fascination for those who came in contact with it. It is probable that the tarantella, which in its present-day form is a lively if rather conventional couples dance with "boldly flirtatious" movements, was originally more sensually abandoned and sexually provocative. In its double image of corruption and virtue, the tarantella might stand as a metaphor expressing the ambivalence of organized society toward the elemental energies and rhythms of dance. For there is surely a subversive element in the natural act of dancing—a note from underground, as it were—which poses a threat to the rules of decorum and the conventions of conformity. "Revelry" sounds much like "revolution" to some; and the drumbeat that drives the dancers carries the throb of the jungle ("the natives are restless tonight").

What is disturbing to orthodoxy is not merely that the rhythmic movement of dance has its analogue, if not its origin, in the act of sexual embrace. It is rather that dancing, like loving, affirms and celebrates an untamed spontaneity in the human, a free spirit, which is intuitively recognized as the enemy of society. Official authority has traditionally held the dance in suspicion; in the Western world the authority of the Church, in particular, was marshaled against nearly all forms of dance for more than a millennium. Even religious dances performed under church auspices were banned for long periods, beginning as early as the sixth century. In a typical action the Council of Avignon decreed in 1209 that, during night watches for the saints, "there shall not be performed in churches play-acting, hopping dances, indecent gestures, ring-dance, neither shall there be sung love-songs or ditties." Not only was the human body to be draped, disguised, and denied; it was to be immobilized. Even more stringent and sweeping prohibitions were later undertaken by the Puritans of New England, who sought to put down gambling, play-acting, and various forms of music as well as dancing. Specifically, the Puritans banned mixed dancing (between men and women), Maypole dancing (considered a pagan rite), dancing in taverns or accompanied by feasting and drinking. A representative tract, issued in 1684 by Puritan ministers in Boston, bore the title *An Arrow Against Profane and Promiscuous Dancing, drawn out of the quiver of the Scriptures.*

The prosecution of the dance and the persecution of dancers failed, of course, not only because of the weakening of ecclesiastical authority but because of the stubborn refusal of ordinary folk to be still. Even in the darkest of ages, in the face of excommunication and the teeth of the Inquisition, the beat went on. It is likely that many of the "diseased dances" of the Middle Ages represented, consciously or unconsciously, expressions of the forbidden rhythmic impulse under circumstances in which violators could appear to be victims. And there were some dances, probably more than have ever been recorded, which plainly mocked and symbolically subverted the hierarchical order of society—a significant case in point being the "Dance of Death" (*Danse Macabre*, or *Totentanz*), widely popular through the Middle Ages, in which Death took the form of a dancer compelling people of all classes, rich and poor, noble and common, to dance with him and be led into the shadows. The Dance of Death was, in effect, says John Martin, "a desperate statement of the common man's disillusionment with the entire social, political, and religious scheme under which he lived; Death leveled all ranks and stations and proved them ultimately vain."

It is generally recognized that the forms of dance prevalent in a society provide a graphic clue to its social character and general culture. But, more than that, they often represent—as do other forms of artistic creation—an active force with a discernible impact of its own on the direction of cultural development. Nor is this true only of the contributions of great innovators, such as Isadora Duncan or Michel Fokine in America; on more than a few occasions the appearance of new popular dances—for example, the waltz and polka in the last century, the jazz dances of the Twenties and Thirties, the rock-and-roll of the Fifties, and the "disco fever" of the Seventies—has approached the stature of a social movement. Less sensationally, but perhaps no less significantly, fashions in dance may reflect a search for roots in ancestral heritages—a stable common ground beneath the diversity and confusion of a fragmented urban culture. Thus, for instance, the square-dance revival of recent years has spread to most parts of the United States and shows no signs of abating.

In the post-rock dance steps of the newly reopened "stardust ballrooms," the beat has become the music, and whirl is king. The rhythm of life comes through loud and clear, conveying the immemorial summons to a ritual enactment of human community. A historian of dance has drawn the irresistible inference: "The strong emphasis on rhythm and beat to the exclusion of melody in this type of dancing is an indication that contemporary teenage social dancing has, in some respects, returned to the beginning of the cycle—to primitive dance, where (in extreme instances) the stamping of feet is the only accompaniment necessary." And something more: the new forms of popular dance appear strongly "to be rooted in a striving for community feeling and group solidarity."

That is not just a backward step for the human art of dancing; it is also its best foot forward.

8 | CULTURE-CROSSING: People-to-People Communication

The awe and dread with which the untutored savage contemplates his mother-in-law are amongst the most familiar facts of anthropology.

—*Sir James G. Frazer*, The Golden Bough

One of the richest contributions of modern cultural anthropology, which the world in general has been slow to assimilate, is the concept of *culture* itself. As distilled by Alfred Kroeber and Clyde Kluckhohn in the 1950s from an extensive survey of prevailing definitions (and couched in the all-too-careful rhetoric of social science), the concept looks as follows:

Culture consists of patterns, explicit and implicit, of and for behavior acquired and transmitted by symbols, constituting the distinctive achievement of human groups, including their embodiments in artifacts; the essential core of culture consists of traditional (i.e., historically derived and selected) ideas and especially their attached values; culture systems may, on the one hand, be considered as products of action, on the other as conditioning elements of further action.[1]

It is difficult nowadays to realize that this fundamental idea concerning the character of culture was scarcely in existence before it was formulated by Edward Tylor in 1871 and very little circulated or understood in the social sciences until at least the 1920s. We were, after all, quite aware in earlier times of the existence of all those different *peoples* (tribes, races, nations) out there in the four corners. In the absence of the culture concept, how on earth did we accommodate and comprehend them?

The answer, of course, is that the Western mind was guided by another and older idea, a proud and magisterial assumption, which the culture concept has gradually displaced and largely discredited—namely, the idea of *civilization*. This grand scheme presented a typological scale of societal evolution, roughly paralleling organic evolution, which ascended steadily upward from "primitive" or "savage" through "barbarian" to "high"—with the last category being (despite a few "classic" exceptions) virtually synonymous with "modern," and that in turn identified exclusively with "Western." There were various definitive indicators—such as logic, law, and literacy—which made it possible to distinguish superior from inferior peoples and to classify all human groups, like captive moths, at various fixed points on the wall chart. The vertical scale of civilization derived its plausibility and credibility (sheer common sense aside) from evolutionary biology, with its sequential organization of life forms from simple to complex; more immediately, the societal scale was grounded in the master idea of the nineteenth century—the idea of *progress*—which

Hegel had logically demonstrated and the Social Darwinists (so it was supposed) had scientifically confirmed. There was also the irresistible evidence of ontogeny (that is, of one's own life): primitive peoples were plainly in the developmental stage of childhood, barbarians were to be regarded as adolescents (and vice versa), while civilized societies had attained maturity (hence were "developed").

Armed with this authoritative measuring stick, any Western observer could venture abroad to dark continents and exotic islands and confidently classify the natives. The method of classification, following natural science, emphasized the similarities within a generic category (e.g., all savages practiced sympathetic magic and were ruled by superstition); differences within the cluster, such as those between separate tribes, were either unnoticed or dismissed as lacking interest. Between civilized and primitive peoples, since they were of different evolutionary orders, there could be little genuine communication—although there could be commerce. What communication was possible consisted mainly of preaching to the natives, and sometimes teaching them, but not listening to or learning from them; in this regard the mode of communication resembled the system of educating the young practiced in Western societies.

The supreme work of this classical school of comparative anthropology was Sir James G. Frazer's *The Golden Bough*, subtitled "A Study in Magic and Religion," which was first published in two volumes in 1890 and later expanded into twelve volumes in 1911–15. This monumental work remains today a mine of fascinating folklore; in its voluminous pages Frazer collected, classified, and interpreted masses of material dealing with such topics as magic, kingship, tree worship, divinity, taboos, totemism, agriculture, rain, fire, and more. The materials were drawn from a vast array of cultures, some of them ancient but many still in existence. Frazer's tales and anecdotes, presented in a superb literary style, may have shed light on the distinctive purposes and patterns of many of these cultures; but what that light might have been we cannot tell from *The Golden Bough*. For Frazer had no field experience in, or firsthand knowledge of, the majority of cultures he dealt with; his research, while it was masterly, was mainly conducted in libraries—and his book, while it was a masterpiece, was a work of historical reconstruction and literary imagination.

The Golden Bough represented, so to speak, the grand climacteric of nineteenth-century armchair anthropology. Even as it was being written, the first generation of cultural anthropologists was in the field—among the aborigines of Australia, the Vedda of Ceylon, the Todas of southern India, the Indians of North and Central America, the Andaman Islanders, and the Trobriand Islanders of the Western Pacific. Of these pioneer explorers of culture it may be said that they came, they saw, and they concurred; that is, they declined to be the agents of cultural imperialism and instead took up an unobtrusive field position as participant observers. They not only came and saw, they stayed; more often than not they remained with a single culture and its people for years, sometimes for decades, and not infrequently for most of a lifetime. When they returned to their home "civilization" in the West, they brought back more than artifacts and anecdotes—they brought a fresh perspective on the cultures of other peoples which carried with it a new appreciation for the complexity, the ambiguity, the artistry, and above all the essential dignity of human communities which, only a generation before, had been collectively categorized as "lesser breeds beneath the law."

BARRIERS DOWN

The barriers to communication between peoples, which not long ago appeared insuperable and permanent, have one by one been knocked down. Cultures once as seemingly impenetrable as those of the remotest tribes of the Amazon or New Guinea, without altogether yielding their cultural autonomy to the pressures of the technologically advanced industrial states, have not been able to escape their influence. In some cases virtually the entire culture has been changed. Students whose parents lived in the Stone Age of New Guinea now attend the university at Fort Moresby. In Manus, in the Admiralty Islands, the whole population has been "Americanized" as a consequence of its occupation during World War II by United States forces.

When the Puritans landed on Plymouth Rock there were well over 300 different Indian cultures in what is now the United States, together with an equal number of different languages. Only a small number of these remain, the rest having been completely destroyed by the hand of the white man, generally with the complicity of the government. It is scarcely surprising that the Indians who remain today think little of white American civilization and that they entertain grave doubts as to whether it can be said to possess any culture at all. One of their principal spokesmen, Vine Deloria, Jr., a Standing Rock Sioux, in a series of brilliant books has challenged white Americans to consider whether they have not more to learn from American Indians than the latter have to learn from them.

Similar views have been expressed among other peoples technologically less advanced but humanly more developed than the "uncivilized West"; and it is a viewpoint more and more encountered in the writings of anthropologists. As Robert Berkhofer has observed, the modern anthropological definition of culture may be seen as a humanistic reaction to modern industrial civilization and a rejection of the crass Social Darwinist evolutionism and scientific racism which have furnished the ideological rationale for economic and political imperialism over colonial peoples abroad and at home. With respect to American Indians specifically, Berkhofer has clearly stated what many anthropologists have intimated— namely, that these so-called "primitives" follow a way of life that is in crucial respects superior to that found in the fragmented cultures of modern industrial societies. In portraying Indian cultures as manifesting the wholeness of humanity, the natural warmth of interpersonal acceptance, and the integrity of organic communion, anthropologists have challenged the values of their own society and repudiated its claim to moral supremacy.

These scientists of man have led us to see culture as that zone of adaptation into which our earliest ancestors moved when they came to rely more and more on learned ways of solving problems. Culture has been defined as the learned part of the environment, or the human-made part of the environment. Although humans are sometimes defined as tool-making animals, there are a number of other animal species which make tools; the tool-making of humans, their technology, is distinguished by the fact that they are the only creatures who make tools with which to make *other* tools, on which they become increasingly dependent for continued existence. Under the general rubric of tools, ideas may well be included. Better, and possibly the best, is the definition of humans as the creatures who communicate through speech. The greatest contribution to the whole subject of speech and language has come to us from anthropologists, who have demonstrated that the best approach to the understanding of another culture is through the study of its language, for language constitutes the formal structure in which a people think. The best exemplification of this perspective is probably still Franz Boas's Introduction to the *Handbook of American Indian Languages*, published in 1911. Not only has nothing more articulate come along; one of the curious things about modern linguistic studies is that while there is much talk of speech and language, hardly anyone has bothered to define them. For example, in a volume entitled *The Role of Speech in Language*, it is assumed that the reader already knows the difference; not one contributor takes the trouble to explain it. There is, of course, a difference. It is possible to have a knowledge of a language, to be able to read and write it, and yet not be able to speak it. On the other hand, it is impossible to speak without having a knowledge of a language. Speech is verbal communication, while language is the body of formal rules governing the use of symbols and signs, be they lingual, vocal, verbal, gestural, or otherwise nonverbal. When one studies both the language and the speech of so-called "primitive" peoples, it is soon found that far from being primitive or backward they are often more complex and refined than any of the languages and ways of speaking of the Western world. Indeed, it is frequently possible to communicate in terms of greater precision and closer meaning in such languages. Every writer in the Western world knows how often it is impossible to find the right word, simply because the language is not refined enough to provide it. Graham Greene spoke for many of us when he pointed to "That long despair of never getting anything right—that *cafard*, that lousiness, that hangs around a writer's life." It is not so with the languages of peoples in the "undeveloped" world; but it requires stepping outside our own system of rules to appreciate their subtleties. For example, Eskimos living in a world of ice have no word at all for that substance—and this has been cited as evidence of their primitive mentality. But ice as such is of no interest to an Eskimo; what *is* of interest, indeed of vital importance, are the different kinds of ice with which he must deal virtually every day of his life. In the same way, the Western anthropologist possesses a substantial filing system dealing with all the branches of anthropology; each of those branches and sub-branches has a file of its own, but there is no file marked "Anthropology." One would be hard put, in fact, to specify what might go into such a file. It would be as useless to the anthropologist as a mental file bearing the label "ice" would be to an Eskimo.

What has been discovered through some fifty years of research is that some languages render their practitioners comparatively inarticulate when matched against the speakers of languages belonging to presumably less sophisticated peoples. Nor is this true only of the languages of these groups; their religions, their kinship systems, their mythologies, and their child-rearing practices are generally so admirably designed to meet the requirements of an integrated everyday life that the modern world has much to learn from them about the ways of civilization. Cross-cultural communication has traditionally been viewed as a unidirectional process—a channel of information, a means of conversion, and a mode of command. As we have indicated earlier, the communication flow was not only one-way but (to Western eyes) downhill—from the "higher races" and mature societies to the "lower" and more "elementary." Throughout the nineteenth century there was hardly a single scientist who was not in this sense a racist. Fortunately, today we no longer hear in these quarters of "higher" or "lower" races; indeed, the term "race" itself has become suspect in scientific circles. Nevertheless, in popular parlance both the term "race" and its equally stereotypic cognate "primitive" continue to be widely used. The employment of such terms in everyday speech evidently pays high dividends; representing as they do pseudological rationalizations based on a medley of unexamined prejudices, such terms enable those who use them to buttress their insecure egos and at the same time to justify their conduct toward the victims of their pejorative labeling. In a vicious circle of prejudice, words become things, things become weapons—and the more weapons one has the more convinced one is of the right to use them.

THE MYTHOLOGY OF "RACE"

The mythology of "race," although it has the sound of something old, is actually a recent development in human history. Before the early nineteenth century it was extremely rare for biology to be invoked as an explanation of the cultural and behavioral differences between peoples. Racism was born in America in the early part of the century when slaveowners found themselves faced with the increasing power of the abolitionists. When squarely confronted with the question whether the slave was not also a man and a brother, the pro-slavers were forced to find answers that would bear exposure—and that would, not incidentally, salve their Christian consciences. The answers they came up with were plain and simple: Yes, the slave was a man, but he was a lesser man; Scripture itself could be cited to show that the black man had been specially created to be of service to his white master. Moreover, the slave was physically different, any one could see that: a creature more closely related to the ape than to the white man, of limited intellectual ability, and originating from the most savage and primitive stock.

For a century and a half this debate has continued. The notion that there is a genetic connection between physical appearance or biological race on one side and intelligence and cultural achievement on the other is known as *racism*. It is this social conception of "race" that is so prevalent in Western societies (Europe, and particularly northern Europe, having been quick to adopt the American invention of the Master Race). The social conception of "race" is not, however, to be confused with either the biological or taxonomic conceptions of race. The biological conception is based on gene frequency distributions or populational differences; the taxonomic conception of race represents a mere classificatory or typological convenience which may, in fact, correspond to nothing whatever in reality.

The mythology of "race" is satisfying to its true believers on various levels. In earlier days people believed as a matter of course in magic, possession and exorcism, in good and evil supernatural powers, and in witchcraft. To judge from the current popularity of books and films on the order of *The Exorcist*, these ancient beliefs are more alive today than many of us had supposed. The credulity of the twentieth century may indeed be as great as it was in earlier days, the difference being merely a shift in emphasis. The witchcraft of our time—the demonology of whole nations such as Germany, Poland, Russia, and Austria, to name but four conspicuous examples—is "race." In the name of "race," the exorcism of the "evil spirits" resident in millions of human beings has been ritually carried out in the ovens and gas chambers of the death camps.

Myths are idealizations of social conditions, given to the function of explaining such things as the origins of differences between people in ways that satisfy the needs of the group. There are, of course, myths of equality and brotherhood as well as myths of inequality and "race." (There is a myth of the Savior, a version of the monomyth of the Hero, which in its Western form has spoken well to the themes of brotherhood, charity, and tolerance.) But there is a resilience to myth, a dense vapor of allegory and parable, which makes it resistant to penetration if not impervious to analysis. It works, like the Deity, in mysterious ways; but it works with great power, and its consequences in the real world are often not mysterious but only awesome. As George Brown Tindall has observed:

Myths [when charged with values, aspirations, ideals and meanings] may become the ground for belief, for either loyalty or defense on the one hand and opposition on the other. In such circumstances a myth itself becomes one of the realities of history, significantly influencing the course of human action, for good or ill. There is, of course, always a danger that in ordering one's vision of reality, the myth may predetermine the categories of perception, rendering one blind to things that do not fit into the mental image.[2]

"Myths," as Paul Gaston has well said, "are not polite euphemisms for falsehoods, but are combinations of images and symbols that reflect a people's way of perceiving truth. Organically related to a fundamental reality of life, they fuse the real and imaginary into a blend that becomes a reality itself, a force of history."

In some nations—for example, Hitler's Third Reich, Rhodesia, South Africa, and Australia, as well as some regions of the United States—the myth of "race" may be seen to function as an ideology. Louis Halle has defined ideologies as doctrines that present themselves as affording a system of belief so complete that whole populations may live by them. An ideology is usually made known and interpreted by leaders ostensibly possessed of special genius or by organized elites, in each case claiming exclusive authority as representing something like revealed truth. In Hitler's Reich, as Leon Wiesaltier has written, "Nothing could more bountifully satisfy the demonological needs of the day than antisemitism. It would be all things to all Germans—a 'scientific' theory of race, a metaphysics, a philosophy of history, an explanation of the modern world, a theodicy and a plan for national regeneration. It accounted for what went wrong and showed how to make it right." Hitler, in fact, thoroughly understood what nonsense his race theory was. In a conversation with Hermann Rauschning, president of the Danzig Senate, the Fuehrer said:

I know perfectly well, just as well as those tremendously clever intellectuals, that in the scientific sense there is no such thing as race. But you, as a farmer, and cattle breeder, cannot get your breeding successfully achieved without the conception of race. And I as a politician need a conception which will enable the order which has hitherto existed on historic bases to be abolished and an entirely new and anti-historic [idea] enforced and given an intellectual basis. . . . With the conception of race, National Socialism will carry its revolution abroad and recast the world.[3]

THE IDEOLOGY OF "INTELLIGENCE"

That version of the myth of "race" has had its night and has failed. But the myth is alive and well in other forms. At the present time there appears to be a recrudescence of interest in determining the role that biological factors—i.e., genetic factors—play in producing "racial" differences in intelligence. Reading the writings of these "scientific racists," one does not wait long to discover the political implication intended to be drawn from their "findings." Society, they tell us, is naturally stratified, the most intelligent rising to the top, the least intelligent sinking to the bottom. The IQ test, it is claimed, is the appropriate diagnostic tool for distinguishing between these natural classes. Once the distinguishing has been done, and the natural inequality of the races established, we can get on to the necessary steps to be taken in the spheres of education, legislation, and resegregation.

Let us take a step backward in time (before returning to this contemporary backward step). Before the development of so-called IQ tests, the biological basis for differences in "racial" intelligence were thought to be adequately proven by the comparative lack of achievement of the "inferior" *vis-à-vis* the "superior" races. After 1916, when IQ tests were beginning to be applied to different "races" in the United States—and especially after World War I, when the results of the Army intelligence tests were published—various studies began to appear which almost invariably claimed to have demonstrated the existence of a genetic factor as responsible for racial or ethnic differences in intelligence. However, as regularly as these studies appeared their conclusions could be shown to be incapable of withstanding critical examination.

To put it the other way around, as often as they have been knocked down these genetic claims have gotten back up and resumed their litany. The most widely discussed argument of this sort in recent years has been that by Arthur Jensen, a professor of educational psychology at the University of California, Berkeley. In an article of 123 pages entitled "How Much Can We Boost I.Q. and Scholastic Achievement?" published in the *Harvard Educational Review* in 1969, Jensen claimed to have found that 80 percent of the 15-point difference on IQ tests between blacks and whites was due to genes and only 25 percent to environment. This estimate has been widely criticized on both methodological and empirical grounds, for there exists no known method of teasing out of the complex expression which is intelligence what role has been played by genes and what role by environment. The most thoroughgoing critique of the hereditarians, and by implication of Jensen's claim, is by Leon J. Kamin, a professor of psychology at Princeton University, in his book *The*

Science and Politics of I.Q. (1974). What Kamin examines are the claims that IQ tests are capable of measuring the heritable contribution to the test results. Kamin shows, as have others before and since, that IQ tests show us literally nothing about heritability. What these tests are able to do is to predict on a better than chance basis who will or will not perform well in existing school training programs. Such tests will also predict, to some extent, who will perform well in our economy and job structure. But that is about all. Among the many weaknesses of IQ tests is that what they are said to measure—namely, intelligence—they do not in fact measure. For the most part IQ test results reflect the effects of socio-economic background and schooling experience. What the test generally tells us is where a child stands in respect of his ability to respond to the test questions as compared with the performance of other children of the same chronologic age. Since, however, chronologic age is itself a poor index of developmental age, the value of the test even from the standpoint of its comparative value is more than questionable. IQ tests are, if anything, likely to be harmful to many children who happen to be slow developers and who, when not condemned to a low IQ status, will catch up with and often outdistance the more rapid developers.

Kamin has stated the conclusion to which all careful investigators can subscribe unequivocally: "To attribute racial differences to genetic factors, granted the overwhelming cultural-environmental differences between races, is to compound folly with malice." And he adds: "The interpretation of I.Q.

data seems never to be free both of policy implications and ideological overtones."

From his own studies Jensen concluded that "compensatory education has been tried and it apparently has failed." As Jensen should know, however, appearances are deceiving; for even while he was drawing his pessimistic conclusion other studies were being conducted which demonstrated the opposite of his claim. The new researches showed the remarkable proficiency of compensatory education in, among other things, raising the IQ of underprivileged mothers as well as of their children by as much as 30 points. These findings have been presented in two reports, one edited by Dr. Sally Ryan, the other written by Professor Urie Bronfenbrenner. Together the two reports—the former containing eight different studies recounted by the investigators and the second presenting authoritative answers to the question "Is Early Intervention Effective?"—constitute a comprehensive rebuttal to those who prematurely claim the death of Headstart and compensatory education programs. What these studies show is that when one breaks through the walls of educational ghettos, which reflect the surrounding ghettos of daily existence, and succeeds in involving the parents in the education of their children (rather than acquiescing in the process of programming them to fail), it becomes possible to transform the school into both an effective center of learning and a focus for community activity and hope. In such schools, reading-score gains average 1.1 years—a full month above the national average; moreover, discipline is improved and vandalism is decreased. The program has, contrary to the claim of Jensen, been strikingly successful. The cumulative evidence indicates that, as E. L. Thorndike remarked many years ago, "To the real work of man—the increase of achievement through improvement of the environment—the influence of heredity offers no barrier."

When environmental conditions are improved, achievement even on IQ tests improves spectacularly. For example, American Indians generally score 80 points on IQ tests. When, however, oil is discovered on their land and they are permitted to share in the profits, their scores in a short time equal those of whites. The oil, it would almost seem, lubricates intelligence potentials that make it possible for Indian children intelligently to enjoy a social and economic environment similar to that of white children. Under such improved conditions among the Osage Indians of Oklahoma, J. H. Rohrer found that on the Goodenough "Draw-a-man" test, the white children scored an IQ average of 103 points and the Indian children an average of 104 points. On a second test, using languages, the white children scored 98 and the Indian children 100. Similarly, Thomas A. Garth found that a group of Indian children living in white foster homes scored an average IQ of 102, whereas the siblings of this group still living on the reservation scored an average of 87.5. Children adopted into socioeconomically favored homes usually do significantly better on IQ tests than their siblings who remain with the biological parents under less favorable conditions.

In 1947 Theodosius Dobzhanky, a geneticist, and Ashley Montagu, an anthropologist, published an

article in which they suggested that every population of the human species, regardless of the different
environments in which they lived, must have been
confronted with much the same challenges, and
therefore their responses, however varied, must have
been of much the same nature. Hence, it might be
expected that *Homo sapiens* everywhere would be
equipped with much the same array of genes for
behavioral development. The same point has since
been frequently made by other scientists. Indeed,
seventy years before Dobzhansky and Montagu published their article the founder of American anthropology, Lewis Henry Morgan, had already an-
ticipated their conclusion. In his book *Ancient Society*
(1877) he wrote: "It must be remarked . . . that the
experience of mankind has run in nearly uniform
channels; that human necessities in similar conditions have been substantially the same; and that the
operations of the mental principle have been uniform
in virtue of the specific identity of all the races of
mankind." It is, in fact, the conclusion of most scientists who have devoted any thought to the matter
that because of the unique evolutionary history of
the human species it is unlikely that there should
exist any major differences in the mental abilities of
the varieties of humanity. Certainly, it is evident
that what the average person can achieve in any society can be achieved by the average human everywhere under similar conditions.

Genes, to be sure, play a significant role in influencing the possible limits of human behavior, but
for those limits or approximations to them to be
reached the appropriate environmental conditions

must be present. It must always be remembered that similarities are not as susceptible of definition as differences and that it is no argument against the likenesses to cite the differences. No two individuals are alike or ever will be, not even miscalled "identical" twins. It is in the differences that the great riches of humanity lie—in the unique and original contribution that each individual is capable of making to family, friends, society, and humanity, when given the opportunity to develop his or her potentialities. If we would preserve our special differences, we must acknowledge our similarities.

The whole question of "race" is in reality a fraudulent one, for it is generally based on a desire to perpetuate inequality of opportunity—in support of which an armamentarium of pseudoscientific "findings" is summoned, allegedly proving the inferiority of a particular group compared with the dominant group. The special pleaders then seek to make their biased evidence the foundation for political and social action which will serve to provide the force and sanction of law to their ideas. Where such views inexorably lead, the entire history of racism serves as a compelling reminder.

Science is on the side of humanity, for its findings fully support the unity of humankind in all its remarkable variety. But the issue of "race" is not a scientific matter; rather it is a problem of ethics, which depends solely on the answer to the simple question: Is this person a human being? If the answer is affirmative, then it follows that he has the inalienable right of all human beings to live his own life, unconstrained and uncategorized, finding his own limits and exploring his unique potential—

experiencing life, enjoying liberty, and knowing the happiness of pursuit. And it follows that any who stand in his way and block his path to self-fulfillment commit the crime of depriving him of his human rights. If that is not the most violent of crimes, it is surely among the most serious in its effect; for to thwart the normal course of a life, to stop its progress and block its growth, is a crime different only in degree from the taking of a life. It is to be hoped that the law, in its imperfect majesty, will one day come to recognize that crime.

Science may play a role in uncovering and testing the facts on which rest, among other things, the claims of the mythologists of "race" (and their brethren the mythologists of "class", defined as a fixed category based on genetic differences). But the matter of rights belongs in the realm of ethics, morals, and finally of politics. Science has much to contribute toward ensuring that every child is born free of physical and mental handicaps; it also has much to provide toward the maintenance of physical and mental health throughout life. Thus science not only has value, it most assuredly has values; but while it serves humanity it cannot subserve politics. On the other hand, what any scientist *does* with his science is another matter, for there he enters into a sphere in which ethical considerations are of predominant concern. So it is with the issue of race and class distinctions. In this area a number of contemporary scientists, like the physicist William Shockley and the psychologist R. J. Herrnstein, would base future political and social action insofar as every individual is concerned on the results of IQ tests. But in cultures of inequality, as we have already seen, IQ tests simply serve to maintain the conditions of inequality. Michael Lewis states the point plainly:

Needing the disinherited, we respond to problems associated with their existence in ways which while frequently promising their alleviation contribute to their persistence. . . . If the problem is poverty, we set about to reform the poor; we do not seriously entertain the possibility of income redistribution and other remedies for economic exploitation. If the problem is race, we may make a few passes at legal redress, but for the most part we bracket race with poverty and concentrate on reforming blacks . . . largely to the exclusion of serious efforts to eliminate those exclusionary practices which make poverty their destiny.[4]

With respect to problems of educational failure, special education is too often emphasized and the backgrounds and brains of the children are made culpable—rather than attending to the more arduous task of reforming the schools and altering the social backgrounds of the children and their families. Similarly, the way we usually deal with crime is to urge more policing of the streets, instead of transforming the social conditions that produce criminals. With the thirty million poor in America, we prefer to deal with devices which seem deliberately contrived to maintain them in their poverty—to keep them down and keep them out. Capitalist democracy has been defined as the form of government which provides every individual, no matter what his origins or socio-economic background, an opportunity to rise by his own efforts—the corollary being that those who fail to rise must have fallen through some deficiency in their character ("the victims of their own vices"). This of course is the supreme cultural rationalization, the secular superstition of a society that seemingly would have us believe—as J. M. Keynes somewhere said of capitalism—that the worst of men from the worst of motives would work for the benefit of all.

Democracy is, of course, in its promise and its principle a form of government which, if not the best that human intelligence and conscience can devise, is at least somewhat less repressive than any other presently known. But democracy can be made to work only if a sufficient number of its members become committed in action as well as in rhetoric to its success. That comes hard for a people to whom "success" has meant merely their own individual victory in a competitive struggle for room at the top. And it comes especially hard when the necessary means to the completion of the democratic experiment involve a substantial element of self-restraint—a recognition that there may be boundaries to acquisition, limits to growth, and diminishing returns in the investment of finite resources toward infinite ambitions. It is not a matter of turning back but of turning away and turning toward. The voice of America has for too long been an inexhaustible monologue addressed to the world at large; the time has come for dialogue across other cultures and within our own. Community requires communication, as John Dewey told us; and communication, for Americans at the crossroads of the future that is upon us, requires attending and listening, approaching and meeting, signalling and touching—and, hopefully, a little learning.

| Notes

CHAPTER 1

1. Edward T. Hall, *The Hidden Dimension* (Garden City, N.Y.: Doubleday, 1966), pp. 130–31.

2. William Sansom, *A Contest of Ladies* (London: Hogarth, 1956), pp. 230–32.

3. Robert Sommer, "Spatial Parameters in Naturalistic Social Research," in Aristide H. Esser, ed., *Behavior and Environment: The Use of Space by Animals and Men* (New York: Plenum Press, 1971), p. 288.

4. David Lowenthal, in *Behavior and Environment: The Use of Space by Animals and Men*, edited by A. H. Esser (Plenum Publishers, 1971), p. 217.

5. Norman Ashcroft and Albert E. Scheflen, *People Space: The Making and Breaking of Human Boundaries* (Garden City, N.Y.: Anchor Books, 1976), pp. 34–35.

6. Sinclair Lewis, *Babbitt* (New York: New American Library, 1961), p. 11.

7. *Ibid.*, p. 26.

8. Jean-Paul Sartre, *Being and Nothingness*, trans. by Hazel E. Barnes (New York: Philosophical Library, 1956), p. 59.

9. *Ibid.*

Chapter 2

1. Weston LaBarre, "Paralinguistics, Kinesics, and Cultural Anthropology," in Floyd W. Matson and Ashley Montagu, eds., *The Human Dialogue* (New York: Free Press, 1967), pp. 463–64.

2. *Japanese Etiquette: An Introduction*, by the World Fellowship Committee of the Tokyo Young Women's Christian Association (Tokyo: Charles E. Tuttle, 1955), p. 6.

3. E. Westermarck, *The Origin and Development of the Moral Ideas*, 2 vols. (London: Macmillan, 1917), vol. 2, pp. 150–51.

4. Erving Goffman, *Relations in Public: Microstudies of the Public Order* (New York: Basic Books, 1971), p. 74.

5. George J. McCall and J. L. Simmons, *Identities and Interactions* (New York: Free Press, 1966), p. 182.

6. Goffman, *Relations in Public*, p. 77.

Chapter 3

1. Edward T. Hall, *Beyond Culture* (Garden City, N.Y.: Anchor Press/Doubleday, 1976), pp. 70–71.

2. William Allen Butler, "Nothing to Wear," in *Harper's Weekly*, February 7, 1857; quoted in *Bartlett's Familiar Quotations*, p. 561.

3. *Ibid.*

4. Quoted in Helmut Morsbach, "Aspects of Nonverbal Communication in Japan," in Larry A. Samovar and Richard E. Porter, *Intercultural Communication: A Reader* (Wadsworth Publishers, 2nd ed., 1976), p. 256.

5. Dolly Martin, *Taffy's Tips to Teens* (New York: Grosset & Dunlap, 1964), pp. 99–100.

6. *Japanese Etiquette: An Introduction*, by the World Fellowship Committee of the Tokyo Young Women's Christian Association (Tokyo: Charles E. Tuttle, 1955), pp. 17–18.

7. Quoted in *Bartlett's Familiar Quotations*, p. 562.

8. *Ibid.*, p. 927.

9. Erving Goffman, *Relations in Public: Microstudies of the Public Order* (New York: Basic Books, 1971), p. 272.

10. Kenneth R. Johnson, "Black Kinesics: Some Non-verbal Communication Patterns in the Black Culture," in Samovar and Porter, *Intercultural Communication: A Reader*, p. 263.

11. T. S. Eliot, "The Love Song of J. Alfred Prufrock," in *A Little Treasury of Modern Poetry: English and American*, edited by Oscar Williams (New York: Scribner's, 1946), pp. 168–73.

12. Norman Ashcroft and Albert E. Scheflen, *People Space: The Making and Breaking of Human Boundaries* (Garden City, N.Y.: Anchor Books, 1976), p. 13.

13. M. Argyle and A. Kendon, "The Experimental Analysis of Social Performance," in L. Berkowitz, ed., *Advances in Experimental Social Psychology*, vol. 3 (New York: Academic Press, 1967).

14. Maurice H. Krout, *Introduction to Social Psychology* (New York: Harper, 1942); chapter on "Symbolism" reprinted in Haig A. Bosmajian, ed., *The Rhetoric of Nonverbal Communication* (Glenview, Ill.: Scott, Foresman, 1971), p. 26.

15. Weston LaBarre, "Paralinguistics, Kinesics, and Cultural Anthropology," reprinted in Floyd W. Matson and Ashley Montagu, eds., *The Human Dialogue: Perspectives on Communication* (New York: Free Press, 1967), p. 466.

CHAPTER 4

1. J. Lionel Tayler, *The Stages of Human Life* (New York: E. P. Dutton, 1921), p. 157.

2. Richard St. Barbe Baker, *Kabongo* (New York: A. S. Barnes, 1955), p. 18.

CHAPTER 5

1. Harry E. Harlow, *Learning to Love* (New York: Ballantine Books, 1971).

2. A fully integrated discussion of our knowledge relating to the importance of love in the healthy development of the individual will be found in Ashley Montagu's three books: *The Direction of Human Development*, rev. ed. (New York: Hawthorn Books, 1970); *On Being Human*, 2nd ed. (New York: Hawthorn Books, 1966); *Touching*, 2nd ed. (New York: Harper & Row, 1978).

CHAPTER 6

1. Norbert Wiener, *The Human Use of Human Beings* (Garden City, N.Y.: Doubleday/Anchor, 1954).

2. Joost A. M. Meerloo, *Conversation and Communication* (New York: International Universities Press, 1952); quoted in Floyd W. Matson and Ashley Montagu, editors, *The Human Dialogue* (New York: Free Press, 1967), p. 146.

3. Erving Goffman, *The Presentation of Self in Everyday Life* (Garden City, N.Y.: Anchor Books, 1959), pp. 3–4.

4. John Lofland, "Interactionist Imagery and Analytic Interruptus," in Tamotsu Shibutani, *Human Nature and Collective Behavior* (Englewood Cliffs, N.J.: Prentice-Hall, 1970).

CHAPTER 7

1. Ray L. Birdwhistell, *Kinesics and Context* (Philadelphia: University of Pennsylvania Press, 1970), pp. 227–28.

2. Edward T. Hall, *Beyond Culture* (Garden City, N.Y.: Anchor Books, 1976), p. 66.

3. J. McLaren, *My Crowded Solitude* (London: Angus and Robertson, 1956), p. 55.

4. Wolfgang Kohler, *Psychologische Forschung* (Leipzig, 1925); quoted in Frances Rust, *Dance in Society* (London: Routledge & Kegan Paul, 1969), pp. 9–10.

CHAPTER 8

1. Alfred Kroeber and Clyde Kluckhohn, *Culture: A Critical Review of Concepts and Definitions* (New York: Knopf, 1963), p. 357.

2. George B. Tindall, *The Ethnic Southerners* (Baton Rouge: Louisiana State University Press, 1976), p. 23.

3. Hermann Rauschning, *The Voice of Destruction* (New York: G. P. Putnam's Sons, 1940), p. 232.

4. Michael Lewis, *The Culture of Inequality* (Amherst: University of Massachusetts Press, 1978), pp. 192–93.

BIBLIOGRAPHY

Aguilera, D. "The Relationship Between Physical Contact and Verbal Interaction Between Nurses and Patients." *Journal of Psychiatric Nursing* 5 (1967), 5–21.

Allport, Gordon W. *Becoming*. Yale University Press, New Haven, Conn., 1955.

Argyle, Michael. *Social Interaction*. Atherton Press, N.Y., 1969.

——, and A. Kendon. "The Experimental Analysis of Social Performance." In L. Berkowitz, ed., *Advances in Experimental Social Psychology*, vol. 3. Academic Press, N.Y., 1967.

Ashcroft, Norman, and Albert E. Scheflen. *People Space*. Anchor Books, Garden City, N.Y., 1976.

Baker, Richard St. Barbe. *Kabongo*. A.S. Barnes, New York, 1955.

Bakwin, Harry. "Emotional Deprivation in Infants." *Journal of Pediatrics* 35 (1949), 512–521.

Barker, Roger G. *Ecological Psychology*. Stanford University Press, Stanford, Calif., 1968.

Berger, Peter L. *Invitation to Sociology: A Humanistic Perspective*. Doubleday/Anchor, Garden City, N.Y., 1963.

——, and Thomas Luckmann. *The Social Construction of Reality*. Doubleday/Anchor, Garden City, N.Y., 1967.

Bergmann, Thesi, with Anna Freud. *Children in the Hospital*. International Universities Press, New York, 1965.

Berkhofer, Robert F., Jr. *The White Man's Indian*. Alfred A. Knopf, New York, 1978.

Berne, Eric. *Games People Play*. Grove Press, New York, 1964.

——. *What Do You Say After You Say Hello?* Bantam Books, New York, 1973.

Bevan-Brown, M. *The Sources of Love and Fear*. Vanguard Press, New York, 1950.

Birdwhistell, Ray L. *Kinesics and Context*. University of Pennsylvania Press, Philadelphia, 1970.

Birenbaum, Arnold, and Edward Sagarin, eds. *People in Places: The Sociology of the Familiar*. Praeger, New York, 1973.

Block, N. J., and Gerald Dworkin, eds., *The IQ Controversy*. Pantheon Books, New York, 1976.

Blumer, Herbert. *Symbolic Interactionism*. Prentice-Hall, Englewood Cliffs, N.J., 1969.

Boas, Franz. "Introduction." *Handbook of American Indian Languages*, part 1.

Bulletin 40, Government Printing Office, Washington, D.C., 1911, pp. 5–83.

Bosmajian, Haig A., ed. *The Rhetoric of Nonverbal Communication*. Scott, Foresman, Glenview, Ill., 1971.

Bowlby, John. *Attachment and Loss*. Basic Books, New York, 1969.

Bowlby, John. *Maternal Care and Mental Health*. Columbia University Press, New York, 1951.

Bowlby, John. "Some Pathological Processes Set in Train by Early Mother-Child Separation." *Journal of Mental Science* 159 (1953), 265–272.

Brady, Terence, and Evan Jones. *The Fight Against Slavery*. W. W. Norton, New York, 1977.

Brazelton, Barry. "Anticipatory Guidance." *Pediatric Clinics of North America* 22 (1973), 533–544.

Brecht, Arnold. "The Myth of 'Is' and 'Ought.'" In *The Political Philosophy of Arnold Brecht*. The New School for Social Research, New York, 1954.

Brenneman, J. "The Infant Ward." *American Journal of Diseases of Children* 43 (1932).

Brody, Sylvia. *Patterns of Mothering*. International Universities Press, New York, 1965.

Brown, Roger. *Social Psychology*. Free Press, New York, 1965.

Bruns, Roger. ed. *Am I Not a Man and a Brother?* Chelsea House, New York, 1977.

Bruyn, Severin T. *The Human Perspective in Sociology*. Prentice-Hall, Englewood Cliffs, N.J., 1966.

Buber, Martin. *Between Man and Man*. Routledge & Kegan Paul, London, 1947.

———. *I and Thou*, 2nd ed. Scribner's, New York, 1958.

Burke, Kenneth. *A Grammar of Motives*. Prentice-Hall, Englewood Cliffs, N.J., 1945.

———. "Dramatism." *Encyclopedia of the Social Sciences*, 1968.

Burling, Robbins. *Man's Many Voices: Language in its Cultural Context*. Holt, Rinehart and Winston, New York, 1970.

Burner, David, Robert D. Marcus, and Jorj Tilson, eds. *America Through the Looking Glass*. Prentice-Hall, Englewood Cliffs, N.J., 1974.

Burns, T. "Non-Verbal Communication." *Discovery* 25 (1964), 30–37.

Butler, William Allen. "Nothing to Wear." *Harper's Weekly*, February 7, 1857.

Carey, James W. "A Cultural Approach to Communication." *Communication* 2 (1975), 1–22.

Chapin, H. D. "A Plea for Accurate Statistics in Infants' Institutions." *Transactions of the American Pediatric Society* 27 (1915).

Cicourel, Aaron. *Method and Measurement in Sociology*. Free Press, New York, 1964.

Clark, Thomas Curtis. "The Touch of Human Hands." In *Bartlett's Familiar Quotations*, 12th ed., edited by Christopher Morley. Little, Brown, Boston, 1951.

Clarke, A. M., and A. D. B. Clarke. *Early Experience: Myth and Evidence*. Free Press, New York, 1976.

Cohen, Albert K. *Delinquent Boys*. Free Press, New York, 1955.

Comte, Auguste. *The Positive Philosophy of Auguste Comte*. Translated by Harriet Martineau. London, 1893.

Condon, W. A., and W. D. Ogston. "Sound Film Analysis of Normal and

Pathological Behavior Patterns." *Journal of Nervous and Mental Diseases* 143 (1966), 338–347.

Condon, W. S., and L. W. Sander. "Neonate Movement is Synchronized with Adult Speech: Interactional Participation and Language Acquisition." *Science* 183 (1974).

Cooley, C. H. *Human Nature and the Social Order.* Scribner's, New York, 1902.

Darlington, Cyril D. *The Evolution of Man and Society.* Simon & Schuster, New York, 1969.

David, Paul R., and Laurence R. Snyder. "Genetic Variability and Human Behavior." In John H. Rohrer and Muzafer Sherif, eds., *Social Psychology at the Crossroads.* Harper & Brothers, New York, 1952.

Deloria, Vine, Jr. *God Is Red.* Grosset & Dunlap, New York, 1973.

de Rougemont, Denis. *Love in the Western World.* Pantheon, New York, 1956.

de Snoo, Karl. "Das Trikende Kind in Uterus." *Monatschrift fur Geburtshulfe und Gynakologie* 105 (1937), 89–97.

Deutsch, Helene. *The Psychology of Women.* Grune & Stratton, New York, 1945.

Dewey, John. *Democracy and Education.* Macmillan, New York, 1916.

———. *Intelligence in the Modern World.* Modern Library, New York, 1939.

Dobzhansky, Theodosius, and Ashley Montagu. "Natural Selection and the Mental Capacities of Mankind." *Science*, 105 (1947), 587–590.

Douglas, Jack D. ed. *Understanding Everyday Life.* Aldine, Chicago, 1970.

Edney, Julian J., and Nancy L. Jordan-Edney. "Territorial Spacing on a Beach," *Sociometry* 37 (1974), 92–104.

Eibl-Eibesfeldt, Irenaeus. "Transcultural Patterns of Ritualized Contact Behavior." In A. H. Esser, ed., *Behavior and Environment: The Use of Space by Animals and Man.* Plenum Press, New York, 1971.

Ekman, P., and W. V. Friesen. "The Repertoire of Nonverbal Behavior: Categories, Origins, Usage, and Coding." *Semiotica* 1 (1969).

Ekman, P., E. R. Sorenson, and W. V. Friesen. "Pan-Cultural Elements in Facial Displays of Emotion." *Science* 164, no. 3875 (1969).

Eliot, T. S. "The Love Song of J. Alfred Prufrock." In Oscar Williams, ed., *A Little Treasury of Modern Poetry.* Scribner's, New York, 1946.

Ellis, Havelock. *The Dance of Life.* Houghton Mifflin, Boston, 1923.

English, Paul Ward, and Robert C. Mayfield, eds. *Man, Space, and Environment.* Oxford University Press, New York, 1972.

Erikson, Erik. *Childhood and Society.* W. W. Norton, New York, 1950.

Escalona, Sybille. *The Roots of Individuality.* Aldine, Chicago, 1968.

———. "Emotional Development in the First Year of Life." In M. J. Senn, ed., *Problems of Infancy and Childhood.* Josiah Macy, Jr. Foundation, New York, 1953.

Esser, A. H., ed. *Behavior and Environment.* Plenum Press, New York, 1971.

Fast, Julius. *Body Language.* Pocket Books, New York, 1971.

Filmer, Paul, Michael Phillipson, David Silverman, and David Walsh. *New Directions in Sociological Theory.* M.I.T. Press, Cambridge, Mass., 1972.

Fraser, John. *Violence in the Arts.* Cambridge University Press, New York, 1974.

Frazer, James. *The Golden Bough.* Macmillan, New York, 1951.

Frazier, Thomas R., ed. *The Private Side of American History: Readings in Everyday Life.* Harcourt Brace Jovanovich, New York, 1975.

Freud, Anna. *Normality and Pathology in Childhood.* International Universities Press, New York, 1965.

Freud, Sigmund. *Introductory Lectures on Psycho-Analysis.* Allen & Unwin, London, 1922.

Fromm, Erich. *The Art of Loving.* Harper & Brothers, New York, 1956.

———. *Man for Himself.* Rinehart, New York, 1947.

———. *The Sane Society.* Rinehart, New York, 1955.

Garfinkel, Harold. *Studies in Ethnomethodology.* Prentice-Hall, Englewood Cliffs, N.J., 1967.

Garth, Thomas R. "A Study of the Foster Child in the White Home." *Psychological Bulletin* 32 (1935).

Gaston, Paul M. *The New South Creed: A Study in Southern Mythmaking.* Alfred A. Knopf, New York, 1970.

Glass, John F., and John R. Staude, eds. *Humanistic Society: Today's Challenge to Sociology.* Goodyear, Pacific Palisades, Calif., 1972.

Goffman, Erving. *Asylums.* Doubleday/Anchor, Garden City, N.Y., 1961.

———. *Behavior in Public Places.* Free Press, New York, 1963.

———. *Encounters.* Bobbs-Merrill, Indianapolis, 1961.

———. *Frame Analysis.* Harper & Row, Colophon Books, New York, 1974.

———. *Interaction Ritual.* Doubleday/Anchor, Garden City, N.Y., 1967.

———. *The Presentation of Self in Everyday Life.* Doubleday Anchor, Garden City, N.Y., 1959.

———. *Relations in Public.* Basic Books, New York, 1971.

———. *Strategic Interaction.* Ballantine, New York, 1972.

Goldfarb, William. "The Effects of Early Institutional Care on Adolescent Personality." *Journal of Experimental Education* 12 (1943), 106–129.

Gordon, Suzanne. *Lonely in America.* Simon & Schuster, New York, 1976.

Gossett, Thomas F. *Race: The History of an Idea in America.* Southern Methodist University Press, Dallas, Tex., 1963.

Gouldner, Alvin W. *The Coming Crisis of Western Sociology.* Basic Books, New York, 1970.

Greenacre, P. "The Eye Motif in Delusion and Fantasy." *American Journal of Psychiatry* 5 (1926).

Gross, Edward, and Gregory O. Stone. "Embarrassment and the Analysis of Role Requirements." In Arnold Birenbaum and Edward Sagarin, eds., *People in Places: The Sociology of the Familiar.* Praeger, New York, 1973.

Gumplowicz, Ludwig. *The Outlines of Sociology.* American Academy of Political and Social Science, Philadelphia, 1899.

Haggard, A. A., and K. S. Isaacs. "Micromomentary Facial Expressions as Indicators of Ego Mechanisms in Psychotherapy." In L. A. Gottschalk and A. H. Auerbach, eds., *Methods of Research in Psychotherapy.* Appleton-Century-Crofts, New York, 1966.

Haire, Doris. *The Cultural Warping of Childbirth.* International Childbirth Education Association, Milwaukee, 1972.

Hall, Edward T. *Beyond Culture.* Doubleday/Anchor Press, Garden City, N.Y., 1976.

———. *The Hidden Dimension.* Doubleday, Garden City, N.Y., 1966.

———. *The Silent Language.* Doubleday, Garden City, N.Y., 1959.

Halle, Louis J. *The Ideological Imagination.* Oxford University Press, New York, 1972.

Haller, John S., Jr. *Outcasts from Evolution: Scientific Attitudes of Racial Inferiority 1859–1900.* University of Illinois Press, Urbana, Ill., 1971.

Hampden-Turner, Charles. *Radical Man*. Schenkman, Cambridge, Mass., 1970.

Harlow, Harry E. *Learning to Love*. Ballantine Books, New York, 1971.

Harrison, R. P. "Pictic Analysis: Towards a Vocabulary and Syntax for the Pictorial Code: With Research on Facial Communication." *Dissertation Abstracts* 26 (1965).

Hearn, Lafcadio. *Japan: An Attempt at Interpretation*. Macmillan, London, 1904.

Hecker, J. F. C. *Epidemics of the Middle Ages*. London, 1835.

Hediger, H. *Wild Animals in Captivity*. Butterworth, London, 1950.

Hendin, Herbert. *The Age of Sensation*. W.W. Norton, New York, 1975.

Henry, Jules. *On Sham, Vulnerability and Other Forms of Self-Destruction*. Random House, New York, 1973.

Herrnstein, R. J. *I. Q. in the Meritocracy*. Atlantic Monthly Press, Boston, 1973.

Heslin, Richard, and Diane Ross. "Nonverbal Intimacy in Arrival and Departure at an Airport." Unpublished manuscript.

Hewes, G. W. "The Anthropology of Posture." *Scientific American* 196 (1957), 123–132.

Howard, H. E. *Territory in Bird Life*. Murray, London, 1920.

Hughes, H. Stuart. *Consciousness and Society*. Vintage Books, New York, 1961.

Hunt, Morton. *The Natural History of Love*. Alfred A. Knopf, New York, 1959.

Husserl, Edmund. *Ideas*. Allen & Unwin, London, 1967.

Hymes, Dell. *Foundations in Sociolinguistics*. University of Pennsylvania Press, Philadelphia, 1974.

Hymes, Dell, ed. *Language, Culture, and Society*. Harper & Row, New York, 1964.

Jackson, Helen Hunt. *A Century of Dishonor*. Harper & Brothers, New York, 1881; reprinted by Harper & Row, New York, 1965.

Jakobson, Roman. "Nonverbal Signs for 'Yes' and 'No.'" *Language in Society* 1 (1972), 91–96.

Jensen, Arthur R. "How Much Can We Boost I.Q. and Scholastic Achievement?" *Harvard Educational Review* 39 (1969), 1–123.

Johnson, Kenneth R. "Black Kinesics: Some Non-Verbal Communication Patterns in the Black Culture." In Larry A. Samovar and Richard E. Porter, eds., *Intercultural Communication*. Wadsworth, Belmont, California, 1972.

Joyce, James. *Ulysses*. Milestone Editions, New York, n.d.

Kamin, Leon J. *The Science and Politics of I.Q.* John Wiley, New York, 1974.

Katsoff, L. A. *The Design of Human Behavior*. Educational Publishers, St. Louis, Mo., 1953.

Kavanaugh, James F., and James E. Cutting, *The Role of Speech in Language*. The M.I.T. Press, Boston, 1975.

Kelley, J. "Dress as Non-Verbal Communication." Paper Presented to the Annual Conference of the American Association for Public Opinion Research, May 1969.

Kendon, Adam. "Some Functions of Gaze-Direction in Social Interaction." *Psychologica* 26 (1967), 22–63.

Kitzinger, Sheila. *The Experience of Childbirth*. Taplinger, New York, 1972.

Klaus, Marshall, and John Kennell. *Maternal-Infant Bonding*. C.V. Mosby, St. Louis, Mo., 1976.

Klineberg, Otto. *Race Differences*. Harper & Row, New York, 1935.

Knapp, Mark L. *Nonverbal Communication in Human Interaction*. Holt, Rinehart & Winston, New York, 1972.

Kockelmans, J., ed. *Phenomenology*. Anchor, New York, 1967.

Kohler, Wolfgang. *Psychologische Forschung*. Leipzig, 1925.

Kraus, Richard. *History of the Dance*. Prentice-Hall, Englewood Cliffs, N.J., 1969.

Krout, Maurice H. *Introduction to Social Psychology*. Harper & Brothers, New York, 1942.

LaBarre, Weston. "Paralinguistics, Kinesics, and Cultural Anthropology." In Floyd W. Matson and Ashley Montagu, eds., *The Human Dialogue*. Free Press, New York, 1967.

Lawrence, R. N. *Date Talk*. Scholastic Book Services, New York, 1967.

Leach, Maria, ed. *Standard Dictionary of Folklore, Mythology and Legend*. Funk & Wagnalls, New York, 1949.

Lemisch, Jesse. "The American Revolution Seen From the Bottom Up." In Barton J. Bernstein, ed., *Towards a New Past: Dissenting Essays in American History*. Vintage, New York, 1969.

Levine, Janey, Ann Vinson, and Deborah Wood. "Subway Behavior." In Arnold Birenbaum and Edward Sagarin, eds., *People in Places: The Sociology of the Familiar*. Praeger, New York, 1973.

Lewis, Michael. *The Culture of Inequality*. University of Massachusetts Press, Amherst, 1978.

Lewis, Sinclair. *Babbitt*. New American Library, New York, 1961.

Lofland, John. "Interactionist Imagery and Analytic Interruptus." In Tamotsu Shibutani, ed., *Human Nature and Collective Behavior*. Prentice-Hall, Englewood Cliffs, N.J., 1970.

Lorenz, Konrad. *On Aggression*. Harcourt, Brace and World, 1966.

Lyman, Stanford M., and Marvin B. Scott. *The Drama of Social Reality*. Oxford University Press, New York, 1975.

Lyman, Stanford M., and Marvin B. Scott, *A Sociology of the Absurd*. Goodyear, Pacific Palisades, Calif., 1970.

Martin, Dolly. *Taffy's Tips to Teens*. Grosset & Dunlap, New York, 1964.

Martin, John. *John Martin's Book of the Dance*. Tudor, New York, 1963.

Maslow, Abraham. *Motivation and Personality*, 2nd ed. Harper & Row, New York, 1970.

———. *Toward a Psychology of Being*. Van Nostrand, Princeton, N.J., 1962.

———. "Our Maligned Animal Nature." *Journal of Psychology* 28 (1949), 273–278.

Masserman, Jules H. *Science and Psychoanalysis*. Grune & Stratton, New York, 1958.

Matson, Floyd W. *The Broken Image*. Braziller, New York, 1964.

———. *The Idea of Man*. Delacorte, New York, 1976.

———, ed. *Being, Becoming, and Behavior*. Braziller, New York, 1967.

———, ed. *Without/Within: Behaviorism and Humanism*. Brooks/Cole, Monterey, Calif., 1973.

———, and Ashley Montagu, eds. *The Human Dialogue*. Free Press, New York, 1967.

May, Rollo. *Love and Will*. W. W. Norton, New York, 1969.

McCall, George J., and J. L. Simmons. *Identities and Interactions*. Free Press, New York, 1966.

McLaren, J. *My Crowded Solitude*. Angus and Robertson, London, 1956.
McLuhan, Marshall. *The Mechanical Bride*. Beacon, Boston, 1969.
———. *Understanding Media*. McGraw-Hill, New York, 1964.
Mead, George Herbert. *Mind, Self and Society*. University of Chicago Press, 1934.
Mead, Margaret. *New Lives for Old*. Wm. Morrow, New York, 1966.
Meerloo, Joost A. M. *Conversation and Communication*. International Universities Press, New York, 1952.
———. *The Dance*. Chilton, Philadelphia, 1960.
———. *Unobtrusive Communication*. Royal Van Gorcum, The Netherlands, 1964.
Melly, G. "Gesture Goes Classless." *New Society*, June 17, 1965.
Merleau-Ponty, M. "What Is Phenomenology?" In M. Kockelmans, ed., *Phenomenology*. Anchor, New York, 1967.
Messinger, Sheldon L., with Harold Sampson and Robert D. Towne. "Life as Theater: Some Notes on the Dramaturgic Approach to Social Reality." In Marcello Truzzi, ed., *Sociology and Everyday Life*. Prentice-Hall, Englewood Cliffs, N.J., 1968.
Miller, G. R., and M. Steinberg. *Between People: A New Approach to Interpersonal Communication*. Science Research Associates, Stanford, Calif., 1975.
Mills, J., and E. Aronson. "Opinion Change as a Function of the Communicator's Attractiveness and Desire to Influence." *Journal of Personality and Social Psychology* 1 (1965), 73–77.
Montagu, Ashley. *The Concept of the Primitive*. Free Press, New York, 1968.
———. *The Concept of Race*. Free Press, New York, 1964.
———. *The Direction of Human Development*. Hawthorn Books, New York, rev. ed., 1970.
———. *The Human Revolution*. Bantam, New York, 1967.
———. "The Language of Self-Deception." In N. Postman, C. Weingartner, and T. P. Moran, eds., *Language in America*. Pegasus, New York, 1969.
———. *Life Before Birth*. New American Library, New York, 2nd ed., 1978.
———. *Man's Most Dangerous Myth: The Fallacy of Race*, 5th ed. Oxford University Press, New York, 1974.
———. *On Being Human*, 2nd ed. Hawthorn Books, New York, 1966.
———. *Prenatal Influences*. C. C. Thomas, Springfield, Ill., 1962.
———. "Social Impacts of Unnecessary Intervention and Unnatural Surroundings in Childbirth." In David and Lee Stewart, eds., *Twenty-First Century Obstetrics Now!* Napsac, Inc., Chapel Hill, N.C., 1977.
———. *Touching*, 2nd ed. Harper & Row, New York, 1978.
———, ed. *Culture and Human Development*. Prentice-Hall, Englewood Cliffs, N.J., 1974.
———. *Learning Non-Aggression*. Oxford University Press, New York, 1978.
Morgan, Lewis Henry. *Ancient Society*. Holt, New York, 1877.
Morris, Desmond. *Intimate Behavior*. Random House, New York, 1971.
Morsbach, Helmut. "Aspects of Nonverbal Communication in Japan." In Larry A. Samovar and Richard E. Porter, eds., *Intercultural Communication: A Reader*. Wadsworth, Belmont, Calif., 1972.
Nesbitt, Paul D., and Girard Steven. "Personal Space and Stimulus Intensity at a Southern California Amusement Park." *Sociometry* 37, (1974), 105–115.
Newman, Grant, and Seymour Levene, eds. *Early Experience and Behavior*. C.C. Thomas, Springfield, Ill., 1968.

Nguyen, T., R. Heslin, and M. L. Nguyen. "The Meanings of Touch: Sex Differences." *Journal of Communication* 25 (1975), 92–100.

——, ——, and T. D. Nguyen. "The Meanings of Touch: Sex and Marital Status Differences." *Representative Research in Social Psychology* 7 (1976), 13–18.

Nicosia, G. J. and J. R. Aiello. "Effects of Bodily Contact on Reactions to Crowding," presented at the 84th Annual Meeting of the American Psychological Association in Washington, D.C., September 1946.

Ortega y Gasset, Jose. *Man and People.* W.W. Norton, New York, 1957.

Ostwald, Peter. "The Sound System of Man." *Communication* 2 (1975), 31–50.

Packard, Vance. *The Hidden Persuaders.* McKay, New York, 1957.

Parsons, Talcott. *The Social System.* Free Press, Glencoe, Ill., 1951.

Pattison, J. E. "Effects of Touch on Self-Exploration and the Therapeutic Relationship." *Journal of Clinical and Consulting Psychology* 40, (1973), 170–175.

Postman, N., C. Weingartner, and T. P. Moran, eds. *Language in America.* Pegasus, New York, 1969.

Psathas, G. *Phenomenological Sociology: Issues and Applications.* New York, John Wiley & Sons, Inc. 1973.

Raiche, B. M. "The Effects of Touch in Counselor Portrayal of Empathy and Regard." Thesis, College of Education, University of Maine, 1977.

Rapoport, Anatol. *Strategy and Conscience.* Harper & Row, New York, 1964.

Raschning, Herman. *The Voice of Destruction.* G.P. Putnam's Sons, New York, 1940.

Rheingold, Harriet L. *Maternal Behavior in Mammals.* John Wiley, New York, 1963.

Ribble, Margaret. *The Rights of Infants.* Columbia University Press, New York, 1965.

Riesman, David, Reuel Denney, and Nathan Glazer. *The Lonely Crowd.* Yale University Press, New Haven, 1950.

Ringer, Robert J. *Winning Through Intimidation.* Funk & Wagnalls, New York, 1974.

Robertson, James. *Young Children in Hospital.* Tavistock, London, 1958.

Rohrer, J. H. "The Test Intelligence of Osage Indians." *Journal of Social Psychology* 16 (1942), 99–105.

Rosenfeld, L. B., S. Kartus, and C. Raye. "Body Accessibility Revisited." *Journal of Communication* 26 (1976), pp. 17–30.

Ruchames, Louis, ed. *Racial Thought in America.* University of Massachusetts Press, Amherst, Mass. 1969.

Ruesch, Jurgen, and Wendell Kees. *Nonverbal Communication: Notes on the Visual Perception of Human Relations.* University of California Press, Berkeley, 1956.

Rust, Frances. *Dance in Society.* Routledge & Kegan Paul, London, 1969.

Ryan, Sally, ed. A Report on Longitudinal Evaluations of Preschool Programs. Department of Health, Education and Welfare Publication No. (OHD) 74-24 and No. (OHD) 74-25.

Sachs, Curt. *World History of the Dance.* W.W. Norton, New York, 1937.

Salk, Lee. "The Effects of the Normal Heartbeat Sound on the Behavior of the Newborn Infant: Implications for Mental Health." *World Mental Health* 12 (1960), 1–8.

Samovar, Larry A., and Richard E. Porter, eds. *Intercultural Communication: A Reader.* Wadsworth, Belmont, Calif., 1972.

Sansom, William. *A Contest of Ladies.* Hogarth, London, 1956.

Sartre, Jean-Paul. *Being and Nothingness*. Trans. by Hazel E. Barnes. Philosophical Library, New York, 1956.

Schaffner, Bertram. *Father Land*. Columbia University Press, New York, 1948.

Scheflen, A. C. "Quasi-Courtship Behavior in Psychotherapy." *Psychiatry* 28 (1965).

Schelling, Thomas C. *Strategy of Conflict*. Galaxy Books, Oxford University Press, New York, 1963.

Schiff, M., et al. "Intellectual Status of Working-Class Children Adopted Early Into Upper-Middle-Class Families." *Science* 200 (1978), 1503–1505.

Schramm, Wilbur, and Daniel Lerner, eds., *Communication and Change*. University Press of Hawaii, Honolulu, 1976.

Schutz, Alfred. *The Phenomenology of the Social World*. Trans. by George Walsh and Frederick Lehnert. Northwestern University Press, Evanston, Ill., 1967.

Schwartz, J. "Men's Clothing and the Negro." *Phylon*, 24 (1963), 224–231.

Secord, Paul F. "Facial Features and Inference Processes in Interpersonal Perception." In Renato Tagiuri and Petrullo, eds., *Person Perception and Interpersonal Behavior*. Stanford University Press, Stanford, Calif., 1958.

Senn, M. J., ed. *Problems of Infancy and Childhood*. Josiah Macy, Jr. Foundation, New York, 1953.

Seward, J. *Japanese in Action*. John Weatherhill, New York, 1968.

Shibutani, Tamotsu, ed., *Human Nature and Collective Behavior*. Prentice-Hall, Englewood Cliffs, N.J., 1970.

Simpson, George G. *Biology and Man*. Harcourt, Brace & World, New York, 1969.

Singer, J. E. "The Use of Manipulative Strategies: Machiavellianism and Attractiveness." *Sociometry* 27:128–151.

Sommer, Robert. *Personal Space*. Prentice-Hall, Englewood Cliffs, N.J., 1969.

———. "Spatial Parameters in Naturalistic Social Research." In Aristide H. Esser, ed., *Behavior and Environment*. Plenum Press, New York, 1971.

Spitz, Rene. *The First Years of Life*. International Universities Press, New York, 1965.

———. *Yes and No*. International Universities Press, New York, 1957.

———. "Anaclitic Depression." *The Psychoanalytic Study of the Child* 2 (1947), 313–342.

———. "Are Parents Necessary?" In *Medicine in the Postwar World: The March of Medicine 1947*. Columbia University Press, New York, 1948.

———. "Hospitalism." *The Psychoanalytic Study of the Child* 1 (1945), 53–74.

———. "Hospitalism: A Follow-Up Report." *The Psychoanalytic Study of the Child* 2 (1947), 113–117.

Steiner, Stan. *The New Indians*. Harper & Row, New York, 1968.

Stevens, S. S. "A Definition of Communication." *Journal of the Acoustical Society of America* 22 (1950), 698.

Suttie, Ian D. *The Origins of Love and Hate*. Kegan Paul, London, 1935; Julian Press, New York, 1952.

Talbot, F. "Discussion." *Transactions of the American Pediatric Society* 62 (1941), 469.

Tayler, J. Lionel. *The Stages of Human Life*. J. Murray, London, 1921.

tenBroek, Jacobus, and Floyd W. Matson. *Hope Deferred: Public Welfare and the Blind*. University of California Press, Berkeley, 1959.

————, Edward N. Barnhart, and Floyd W. Matson. *Prejudice, War, and the Constitution.* University of California Press, Berkeley, 1954.

Thayer, S., and W. Schiff. "Stimulus Factors in Observer Judgment of Social Interaction, I. Facial Expression and Motion Pattern." City College of the City University of New York, 1967.

Tiryakian, Edward A. *Sociologism and Existentialism.* Prentice-Hall, Englewood Cliffs, N.J., 1969.

Tisdall, George B. *The Ethnic Southerners.* Louisiana State University Press, Baton Rouge, 1976.

Truzzi, Marcello, ed. *Sociology and Everyday Life.* Prentice-Hall, Englewood Cliffs, N.J., 1968.

Ueda, Keiko. "Sixteen Ways to Avoid Saying 'No' in Japan." In *Patterns of Communication In and Out of Japan.* International Christian University, Communication Department, 1971.

Van Emery, Dale. *Disinherited: The Lost Birthright of the American Indian.* Wm. Morrow, New York, 1966.

Vaud, Gaston. *Intelligence: Its Evolution and Forms.* Harper & Row, New York, 1960.

von Cranach, Mario. "The Role of Orienting Behavior in Human Interaction." In Aristide H. Esser, ed., *Behavior and Environment.* Plenum Press, New York, 1971.

Walster, E., et al. "Importance of Physical Attractiveness in Dating Behavior." *Journal of Personality and Social Psychology* 1 (1965), 184–197.

Washburn, Sherwood L., and C. S. Lancaster. "The Evolution of Hunting." In Richard B. Lee and Irven DeVore, eds., *Man the Hunter.* Aldine, Chicago, 1968.

Watson, John B. *Behaviorism.* University of Chicago Press, 1958 (original edition 1924).

Watson, O. Michael. *Proxemic Behavior: A Cross-Cultural Study.* Mouton, The Hague, 1970.

Westermarck, E. *The Origin and Development of the Moral Ideas,* 2 vol. Macmillan, London, 1917.

Whorf, Benjamin. *Language, Thought and Reality.* John Wiley, New York, 1956.

Whyte, W. F. "When Workers and Customers Meet." In W. F. Whyte, ed., *Industry and Society.* McGraw-Hill, New York, 1946.

Wiener, Norbert. *The Human Use of Human Beings.* Doubleday Anchor, Garden City, N.Y., 1954.

Wieseltier, Leon. "History and the Holocaust." *Times Literary Supplement* (London), February 25, 1977.

Wolfe, Tom. *The Pump House Gang.* Bantam, New York, 1969.

Wolff, Kurt H., ed., *The Sociology of Georg Simmel.* Free Press, Glencoe, Ill., 1950.

Wolff, Michael. "Notes on the Behavior of Pedestrians." In Arnold Birenbaum and Edward Sagarin, eds., *People in Places.* Praeger, New York, 1973.

Woodcock, George. "The Lure of the Primitive." *The American Scholar* 45 (1976), 387–402.

Wrong, Dennis. "The Oversocialized Conception of Man in Modern Sociology." *American Sociological Review* 26 (1961), 183–193.

Yerkes, R. M. "Psychological Examining in the United States Army." *Memoirs of the National Academy of Sciences* 15, 1921.

Zunin, Leonard, with Natalie Zunin. *Contact: The First Four Minutes.* Nash Publishing, Los Angeles, 1972.

INDEX

Catalog

If you are interested in a list of fine Paperback
books, covering a wide range of subjects
and interests, send your name and address,
requesting your free catalog, to:

McGraw-Hill Paperbacks
1221 Avenue of Americas
New York, N.Y. 10020